**This book is made
in the presence of
good vibes.**

ALSO BY LARA JAY HEQUET

Excuse Me,
May I Ask You
A Question?

How To Ask Questions
That Will Change The
Way You Live

Right To Write Publishing

London | Singapore

www.righttowritepublishing.com

ONCE UPON A TIME A TIME I WOULD GROW OLD

Life-Changing Ideas
55 Practices and
Inspirations to Guide You from
the Act of Growing Older to
The Art of Living Older

LARA JAY HEQUET

Disclaimer

The words and ideas in this book have come to me in living a roller coaster life the best way possible. These are ideas I am designing for my own *Living Older* journey. I intend to live this journey to the best of my ability right up until the next transition whatever it may be.

The words and the ideas in this book are not based on research accomplished by a limited-sized room full of people. I believe that the human spirit is too unique for research to represent it in its entirety using controlled answers or proofs. Instead, I believe that as human beings we are beautifully complex, and much larger than what the mind alone can understand.

This book is not meant to be taken as advice or to replace medical advice or any current belief you have concerning health or ageing. It is an idea that is personal to the author. It is an idea that you, the reader, may play with and enjoy within the realms of your mind, body and soul. If you spot any mistakes within the book, we would love to hear from you; however, remember to enjoy the true creative experience and inspirations it is offering you.

No animals or people were hurt, nor were caves, where I was writing, ruined during the writing process.

In Consideration, Gratitude and Love

This book is for the very brave.

The ones with crazy, magic dust sprinkled all over them.

Those not easily deterred from their true selves.

The ones who will step up.

Step up to celebrating life.

Until the very end of this physical journey.

Leaving behind a better place than we knew it.

Just because we lived big.

In consideration of those who have gone before us and those who will follow us.

Moving forward towards the unknown journeys of our very wild souls.

This book is also for the less brave.

Those who have as yet to unleash.

The power to be a One that counts.

For any great movement in numbers.

Starts with the very little One.

To my loving Q and A.

There is not one hindrance, nor is there an excuse not to shine your individual light as bright as it needs to shine on your life journeys. I thank you for cherishing my wild soul. I am blessed, honoured and in deep gratitude to have you both choose me to be your mother on the journey of your life.

To my large and loving family.

Thank you for always extending to me your home and your shoulders for me to rest on after my wild journeys. I am able to fly because you ground me with your love and laughter.

To my friends of all different shapes, sizes, beliefs and colours from all parts of this beautiful world.

I thank you for entering my world and for sharing your individual magic which sparks my wild fire to do better, and to be better, for myself, for you, and for all whom I have yet to know.

Dear reader.

It is possible that we once exchanged smiles on 'The Tube' in London, on the streets of Dublin and Galway, in the city of Bonn and on the little hidden streets of Singapore.

Am I a natural writer?
Perhaps not.
But a message,
I do have to share.
A question to ask,
A wonder to initiate,
A topic to stir,
A change to make,
A better life to live,
A greater one to end.

Always.

A Menu Of Contents

_ to Savour

A Menu of Poetry

_ *to Guide*

A Key of Contents

_ to Seek

Ideas and Suggestions

Practice and Exercises

Gratitude and Thanks

Who Am I?

I am you.

I am the person who walks on the streets

where homeless people lie.

I go to malls when I am self-indulgent and

when I have lost my sense of purpose.

I have worries and I have fears

which surface only to be dealt with

so that they may quiet down.

These examples and many others

make me like you, dear reader, a human being of today.

In this world and way of being, I am connected.

I feel my soul.

I feel it alive and growing

with the experiences that are my life.

This drives me with a yearning not to be sick,

to look after myself,

to be a better person.

Are you me?

Preface

It is time to change the way we look at growing old and all of its negative implications and associations. My love for life led me to write this book from the depths of my heart as I prepare for the natural change in seasons of the circle of life. I have chosen not to rely on research from other sources, since my personal experiences provide the basis for my journey into **Living Older**. Statistics, including its limitations in researching life and the human spirit as a holistic form are 'not my thing'. In my opinion, they do not provide a pathway of newness, and they can never cover the entirety of beautiful individuals and animals living on this planet. Of course, there are always exceptions. In this space of personal stories and ideas, existing facts and any research in this subject matter are respected; however, they are not considered.

My intention is to call out to other like-minded individuals who believe that life is, indeed, beautiful. And as such, why does the idea begin to fade while we become older but are still very much living? This description of beauty is inclusive of every dark and unhappy moment that plays an important role in both a tumultuous and a wholesome life. Every step of the journey, from being born to passing on, is one of ceremonious dignity, evolving purpose, and individually expressed beauty.

It is a book that is shared so that minds are stirred. Whether this book is loved or not loved is not the objective. The stirring of emotions relating to *Living Older* is what will drive us towards a change. It is not a book of answers or miracle cures to anything. At its roots, it is a book full of soul that awakens us to what we already know deep inside of us to be the truth.

Five objectives have been achieved since the beginning of this writing journey. Objective one – *Once Upon A Time I Would Grow Old*, the book, is written and published. Objective two – The book introduces an option as a way of being described as *Living Older* that is available to all of us, but is in need of being excavated like a priceless artefact buried for a long time. Objective three – The conceptualisation of WOWAGEING™ , to house the idea of *Living Older* instead of growing older introduced within this book for real-time interaction during organised events, both online and live, to provide growing information, continuous learning and social fun. Objective Four – The set-up of wowageing.com, an online community portal for like-minded people from all over the world. It will serve as a support system as well as an information system for progress in making the positive and necessary changes while walking new paths that could be rough. It will also provide relevant and positive habit forming online and onsite courses related to possibilities in *Living Older*. Objective five - Invite interested readers to join wowageing.com as a community member. Be a vital part of its growth by creating new paths in choosing to *Live Older*. As a community member, receive more information relating to special themed events, workshops and travels that will further elaborate how to make the practices work for the individual or groups of people.

Of course, this work is only the beginning.

Once Upon A Time I Would Grow Old is a book that may dig up our buried emotions so that they begin to ignite. It is an inspirational book that may bring to the surface a new energy and new ways of being, which encourage the self-designed adventures of a wild-crafted living process. There is an urgent need for a movement to change the way we look at growing old and all of its current, mostly negative, implications and associations. The focus lies in looking towards a continuous and purposeful love of life while we are living, rather than anticipating a time of inevitable sickness and the impending, largely negative, end of the physical life.

The book includes an introduction of new and created words throughout the writings.

These words will be highlighted in bold. Please refer to **New Dictionary for WOWAGEING™** in Appendix i for their elaborate definitions.

Together, we will create a dynamic movement that will inspire us to do a lot more in time while we have fun and savour each breath of life as if it were the last.

Enjoy the creative ride!

Ordinarily, we have the choice to sit in a room full of darkness and complain about how dark it is

or

we have the choice to get up to switch on a light that was always present in the darkness.

The choice we make could change the entire perspective.

Extraordinarily, we could find ourselves in a room that does not have a light switch.

In this case,

one could truly experience the importance of light

and use this energised passion to get up and create light out of unseen elements within the darkness.

In The Beginning

My Body or My Soul: What is Driving My Life?

I have a soul. I recognised its exuberance at the age of six. Of course, at that point I had no real idea that everyone else had a soul, too. It was not a mental thought that goes around and around in your head as things start to do when you grow older.

It is easy to hold as true any belief when you are young. I am an ordinary human being that has an extraordinary perception of life. I have the knowledge of many great civilisations in my blood. I speak many languages, most of which I learned when I was too young to choose them for myself.

At six, I remember standing on the top of a high mountain that happened to be the location of my boarding school. I cried my heart out, having declared and held true that my parents were dead. What other possible reason had they sent me to this faraway place? In truth, however, my parents were not dead, and they had not abandoned me. They reasoned that they were giving me the best in terms of education. Of course, it was not something I could understand at the time. In my mind and heart my declaration rang true.

This is when I was first introduced to my soul. Of course, I was not a saint so I did not call it a soul. I just knew it to be something special, and I could sense that it was there with me—all the time. During this very early time in my life,

I felt a strong connection that assured me that all would be all right. It was time to lay my sadness to rest with my declaration. It was time to begin to look forward and proclaim my presence in this world.

Even then, in the midst of the highest mountains, I was striving to live a life of freedom, albeit in my own head.

At the age of nine, I tried to run away from the boarding school with a dedicated tribe of three cohorts, even though there was really and truly nowhere to go. Although we were caught and punished, we tried again and again to run away. I did not have far to run, but the two hundred meters felt epic as the first of many adventures in my life that were about to unfold. At an unknown time, I subconsciously made a decision to find other ways to achieve this freedom. I did not have far to go, but the two hundred meters felt epic as the first of many adventures in my life that were about to unfold.

Everything I have done since this time has been performed with an unintended rebellion against the accepted social norms. After graduating from hotel school, I turned down opportunities to work at the best and biggest hotels. Instead, I chose to work on remote islands where conditions were much less comfortable. Though I was a hard-core urbanite, I chose to venture forth to more challenging environments outside of my comfort zone. Looking back, I came to see how following intuitive decisions to not conform result in great flavours that can enhance the recipe for a great life.

My refusal to choose a particular career caused a lot of trouble for those close to me, who felt I lacked focus. But I ignored the criticisms of naysayers, opting instead to pick up a wide range of useful skills. My strategy was driven by passions that were vast and varied. Each one of my passions that were stirring inside me wanted the spotlight for something special in this life.

I have committed to long-term love twice in my life. Both relationships have brought me two amazing children. Eventually, I ended the partnerships because I knew that it was time to move on. Due to circumstances bigger than love, staying on would have only hurt our beautiful and individual souls.

I was diagnosed with cancer and survived. I was prepared to die an early death by concentrating on living, even if for a few days, instead of surrendering to the suffocating veil of fear that comes with the imminent prospect of dying.

I have never had too much money or owned anything other than my skills, but I have been surrounded by many people who do. I see how too much money or too little of it takes over a life of a human being. I have always found money when I really needed it to put food on the table. I have been an employee of large businesses and I have been the employer of very small businesses.

I have experienced many fears that invited themselves into my head. I have amazed myself with what I have been able to overcome, despite the on again, off again residency of these fears. As my life journey has progressed, I have learnt to be aware, to observe, to watch, and to understand my place, at any given moment, in silence. This practice has allowed me to discover a large palette of many colours that provides me with the capacity to become a continuously evolving human being. The ability to celebrate my life in times of adverse and compelling challenges has become a necessity that stretches any limitations of my purpose on this planet.

I have a sense of gratitude for the new challenging experiences that bring me lessons to stretch myself even further. My soul carries a deep inner voice that pushes my physical and mental limits, guiding me to stay quiet if need be. The voice helps me see the world in all of its depths.

When I was younger, this voice scared me sometimes. What I could sense was often beyond my physical being, and the scope of my mental comp-rehension. This voice—my soul—has accompanied me in a life of many adventures and ways of being. Best of all, this voice of my **wild soul** fits me perfectly today. With increased years, my physical and mental beings seem to be catching up with its vastness.

In continuous gratitude for the life I have lived and still live, why would I move toward the ending chapters of my physical life as if my soul had already expired? If my life truth has understood and accepted that life is a full circle, I will have no need to deny my body and mind the right to change as they gloriously prepare for the final stage in this life journey.

You see, dear reader, I realise that I do own a soul and that it is exuberant. I also know that it is wild and free. My wild soul is here for the ride . . . the ride that is my life. It is up to me to make the very most of this journey, one that does not end because of a given status to a number or numbers at any physical age. I commit and dedicate my life to living with the largeness of this spirit, to live it wild, free and purposeful, to live it in the uncertainty that is its condition. I intend to live it until my soul is ready to fly out of the physical realm that has been its home.

Is there anyone else out there who feels the same?

DEAR READER,

The main objective of the information herein is to 'kick ass', mostly my own, but perhaps yours, too.

———

If this book does the least bit of good, it will be to remind you that you are not yet 'dead', a truth we have a tendency to forget very quickly. So get up, light your fire and make this world a better place! Keep going until the lights of your physical world turn off.

NO EXCUSES. ABSOLUTELY NONE!

The word 'weird' uttered from the mouth of an ordinary human being makes so much sense to the ears of human beings who are truly more than ordinary.

I will look as I have lived.
Full of stories in the freedom of my many emotions.
My soul will be, more than ever,
Heard through the words I choose to speak

2

When I Got to The Top of 'Over-the-Hill'

I know that I am not the only one afflicted with the apparent 'malady' of growing older. Before I turned fifty, the idea of growing older was slowly making noises that were heard inside my consciousness. It was not a nagging call from the deep insides of my head, but rather, noises that came from my vast and versatile environment; the messages they conveyed were about how everything was going to change for the negative.

Many of these messages were common, suggesting that life would be a downhill slide no matter what you did or tried to do. However, the deeply guided thoughts in my spirit had a different musical calm. The tune carried a different lyric. If death is a natural part of life, then surely I would be alive and living right up until I actually physically died. This music in my ears was a tune that set me apart from many others in my environment, and reflected a vastness that included several different cultures on the planet.

One of the revelations in knowing that you are special is when you are proudly able to proclaim that you are weird. It means that you are different from the masses and the generalisations that pollute our breathing space.

As I became more interested in placing my curious eyes and ears on the reality of growing older, the meaning of ageing seemed to be synonymous

with aches and pains, illness, disability, loneliness and other not so great scenarios. In my observations, the generations before me were growing old in ways that did not seem acceptable to me. My parents, and others of their generation, though stemming from different cultures and countries, shared a common language both linguistically and bodily: they were old, had illnesses, and they were no longer of usefulness. The jury, which included themselves, had decided that they were old long before they were actually old.

What was their definition of 'old'? Old seemed to mean that they were somehow dependent, not because they were old as we are naturally designed to be, but because their life and existence was stripped of any useful purpose.

This dependence was interpreted to mean that they were a burden, and that their Self was imprisoned within their own bodies and mind. Growing older was a heavy weight no one would bear with any joy, or so we became to believe. If the dependency was not on another person, then it was on a medication or a social benefit. More importantly, the dependence was related to an unavoidable and seemingly unacceptable way of being—a curse for any human being who lives with ego in full gear. It was no wonder that everyone wanted to remain young forever!

If, for example, Candidate Older were to run for president with slogans such as 'Over-the-Hill', 'Retired', or 'Uncool', the candidate would be taken out to pasture, while Candidate Younger ran with slogans such as 'Dynamic', or 'Full of Ideas'; clearly, Candidate Younger would have more appeal.

Did this mean that older is simply and naturally measured only by its chronological age? It could not be as simple as that. I know this to be true because I work with young people who are already old in their young bodies, not due to an illness, but because of choice in lifestyle and attitude.

The term 'over-the-hill' was the phrase du jour to explore when approaching the environs of my forties. I looked forward to seeing these notorious 'hills' by the time I turned fifty, thinking that I may have been an extended delinquent who missed seeing them in my forties, while I was busy living a fulfilling life.

In all honesty, I was a little apprehensive as I consciously searched for these hills. When fifty arrived, the only hills I saw were hills that I had seen earlier on in life. These were the same hills representing the different challenges that needed to be 'climbed' if I wanted to get anywhere. And yes, I was still going places on new journeys and familiar hills.

More important to me than the new hills I was climbing was the ocean of endless possibilities.

My soul and I knew right then and there that I would be fine when setting forth on whichever journey I take. All that would change would be what needed to change as a natural result of this journey that we call life. Neither fighting the omnipresent phase of growing older, nor hiding from it is a part of my journey. I will live beautifully until the lights in my physical and mental body switch off. When and how this may happen is not where I direct my energy.

I will accept this magical gift of not needing to know, as it is designed to be.

3

Rolling Down the Hill Uncontrollably or Surfing It?

As a grand gesture to the opening story of my *Living Older* journey, I decided to pack up my eleven-year-old daughter with her online school programme, and leave behind everything I knew to be comfortable, familiar and financially stable. I was determined to observe with more intention my growing older life, and the growing older lives of others with a 'switched on' consciousness. I wanted to be wilfully prepared for a new way of being that was coming on fast, so as to live the rest of the best and grandest years of my life leading up to a well-organised finale.

When I turned fifty, I decided to pave the way for a more celebrated and more colourful way to living the rest of my life. I felt a yearning to write this book, so I embraced it as I travelled to unknown environments and strange destinations for the very first time. I decided to write the book in an authentic voice, the voice with which I actually live my life. I did not want to use words that are not the way I speak, or to adopt a vision that is not the way I see life. The stories, information, thoughts and perceptions compiled in this book are not meant to be preachy. If they have a tendency towards being preachy, it is only because the thoughts that come to me enlighten me to such high notes. If you come across them, lighten up, imagine a big halo around your head and enjoy the moment.

4

Why is Becoming Older Such a Bad Thing?

" When I was
   younger... "

" I was so good looking
   when I was younger. "

" I will lose my
   memory. "

Upon starting this journey in *Living Older*, the first discovery I made through my observations is that everyone grows older.

The second discovery I made is that many 'bodies' pretend that they are not growing older.

Is it possible that growing older has been manipulated to represent the end of everything we have loved and enjoyed about ourselves being human?

Here are some examples of overheard, over-read and over-lived statements concerning growing older:

" You do not look
  your age. "

" That's the end of
  my sex life! "

" Growing older is
  boring and way
  uncool! "

It is no wonder
growing older sounds
like a terrible, contagious
affliction. Thanks to such
non-sensical thoughts
and ideas, older age is
like a horrible and cursed
destination everyone
wants to avoid.

" I feel depressed
  as I wait to die. "

" Oh, (groan) I ache
  and I am in pain."

" There is no
  more fun. "

" I will lose all of
  my faculties. "

" I am too old
  for that. "

" What is the point
  of living? "

" Back in the good
  old days... "

Facts, Myths, Beliefs and New Thoughts concerning Ageing:

1.

Why is it that at the start of a life cycle, we joyfully entertain and care for a little baby who cannot fend for itself, but we surround an elderly person who is about to complete the journey with doom, darkness and loneliness?

2.

Growing older is as natural as a baby's first cry and the many more cries that come with being alive. And it is just as natural that life designs with drawings of wrinkles and colours of grey, white and silver. It is a time of celebration for a life that is very much alive and still being lived.

3.

Our physical bodies are like houses that need care: fixing leaks, rewiring, painting new coats of paint. The older the house, the more care it may require. This does not change the spirit of the people who choose to live in this house. The charm of old houses is becoming a rarity in the fast and overly developed world in which we reside.

4.

An ageing life, and the expiry of its worthiness, can no longer be based solely on the value and the timeline of corporate employment.

5.

If a baby represents hope for the future, growing old represents the value of a life that has lived its story, whatever the plot.

6.

What would the interpretation of a society be (in one word or sentence) when the young have no sense of earning, and therefore spend ruthlessly, while the elderly are hired to do the cleaning jobs that no one else finds of value to do?

7.

Birth is a celebration— a time of utter happiness in the continuity of life, love, care and genes. Old age, on the other hand, seems like imprisonment in a physical and mental being that is limited, disabled and full of pain.

8.

Images of being controlled and constrained in homes and facilities where one waits to die tend to be pasted into our subconscious when interpreting the meaning of an older life.

9.

Once upon a time we were all toddlers—weak on our knees as we started to walk. Our parents could not help but think of us as 'cute and adorable', with pride in each of our new landmarks of progress. On the other side of the life circle, when an older person, perhaps our parents, are wobbly on their knees, why do we have a tendency to think of them as weak, frail, old, and burdensome?

10.

Why is growing old handled mostly as a liability or a disease we would rather not talk about? Yet, we all have to grow old, no matter whom or what we are: man, woman, rich, poor, educated, uneducated, healthy, unhealthy, leader, follower, winner, loser, queen, king or pauper.

11.

Emotionally, we are locked up because not many of us want to talk about death.

We cannot be dead while we are still alive, unless we made a choice to be so.

The design of one's life is a set of variables that can be changed with a personal commitment to how we will choose to live it at any given moment. Once upon a time, each of us was born, was a child, was young; now we are adults who are continually growing older, until, eventually, we die. We all know this to be true. Why then do we live our lives as if we are ignorant of this truth? At death, depending on our individual beliefs or stories, our souls may move on to a different place, cycle, or continue on in our journey. Whatever happens then is certainly of no concern to our needs in living right now. The circle of life is a celebration of the entire circumference of the circle. There is no fine print that states older age is to be excluded.

Old age is not a curse that befalls humanity. It is a part of being alive that is necessary in the circle of life. It may not be a time of physical prowess, or for reproduction. Nonetheless, it is certainly a time of rich experiences (if chosen), lively wisdom (if sought) and abundant spirituality (if connected).

When ageing is viewed through a small and narrow lens, disabilities are the only thing that come into focus. The real and simple truth is that ageing provides an accumulation of experience and wisdom. It deserves the right of respect and to be treated as a valuable asset within a community, rather than being labelled a burden on which a society is built.

It is disrespectful to the magical journey of life when we pick and choose what to highlight based on what is currently pleasing to the masses, and on what is profitable to a limited few. The generation of us brought up on rock 'n' roll, freedom, and individuality, needs to use a different set of observations and discoveries to create a new definition of growing older, and to pave a relevant and positive pathway for ourselves and for the generations who will follow. It is time to stop all limited concepts concerning ageing. Indeed, it is time to **fashionise** ageing (to create individual expression so cool that everyone wants to try it).

It is time to walk the talk. This is not about creating a one-size-fits-all belief in growing older. It is about creating a path to a good life right up until death and separation from the physical body and mind.

The value of a completed life lies in how it was lived; it does not lie solely on a number we allocate to be representative of an age.

Maybe yes?
Maybe no?

I, for one, will move in the direction of yes!

The Fountain of Youth

The Fountain Of Youth
is sought by some.
An entire lifetime will pass in its search.
I have lived my life
as a droplet flowing
into a stream,
into a river
through rapids
and wide, turbulent waterfalls.
Towards
the never-ending vast and unknown depths
of the ocean
is where I seek to go!

A Side Story

I decided to take up a yoga teacher training class at the age of fifty-one. I am generally physically active, but I had never attended an official yoga class. I was sitting for a class project among a group of women mostly in their early twenties. One of the girls said, 'Younger people like faster, stronger things. Old people like slower things, quieter things'. The girl did not know much of my life story, just as I did not know hers. However, it seemed so easy to settle into this generalisation without questioning the actual individual (myself) on whose behalf she was apparently speaking.

Such a generalisation is made just because it is made; it is a belief because it is a belief, adopted or comfortably worn without much thought or discernment.

The situation, as well as the entire training period, ended up being an opportunity for me to share with her the extent of how misinformed she really was in her beliefs. The truth is that there are all kinds of people who like all sorts of different things. Yet, no matter how often our beliefs limit us, there is no one ready-made template that will fit all of humankind.

Make time to know the difference, and to experience every life form for its individual Self.

Youth is but one phase of an eternally revolving cycle. This circle of life is unique for each soul that lives within it. As the circle goes up and down, like a ball, through the holistic roller coaster of life, it would be very limited to believe that one stays at any one point of this spinning circle all the time. Every time, living is to experience every important offering within this circle to be an incomparable phase in the journey that is life. With which we live an entire life as reference. Without which we will agree that each phase had it's share of experienced memories. And being who is living each phase worthy of a life well-lived will agree that each phase serves marketeers of wares and services in need of tools and reasons for exploitation in using our fears and our regrets. Our conscious presence in a life that is ours is the only fuel we need to live big.

The artificial 'inflatedness' of any phase serves marketeers of wares and services in need of tools and reasons for exploitation in using our fears and our regrets. Life is not only about living. Every time. As the circle goes up and down, like a ball. The purpose in living is youth.

5

Coming Out of the Dazzling Rabbit Hole of Un-Needed Wants In The Land of More More More

Q What do we hear and observe most in our environment concerning ageing and being older?

A 'Anti-ageing', a powerful expression that implies feelings of negativity and hate. The prefix 'anti' has a connotation of being truly, strongly and absolutely against someone or something. Remaining in this context would suggest that ageing must be a negative process or a way of being that we need to resist, hate, or avoid at all costs!

Anti-ageing attitudes drive an invisible bent of negativity into our subconscious minds as we go about our daily commuting, buying and reading in a world full of options, perhaps with too many options. Our senses are constantly ignited and reignited before we can fully process the pleasures of the previous pleasure. Equally, our troubles are flash-ignited and quickly buried before we have the opportunity to face them, to cry over them, and to deal with them as a vital part of a larger life journey.

Everything is designed to be faster, more exciting, better looking, easier to use and easier to throw away. It is no wonder that our beautiful planet is dis-eased. We are able to like a person or a product based on how enticing it appears without even trying it first. Why do we fall prey so easily to corporate media telling us what they want us to believe? It may be that we have forgotten the art of loving ourselves and caring for ourselves. We may have buried our consciousness and put aside the innate knowledge of what our individual bodies need at any given moment. We may have surrendered our unique abilities to be owned by those more compelling with their voices. We begin to conform to their existing templates in order to receive a generic stamp of approval.

We are surviving in a material world where our minds and ways of being are studied in order to be manipulated for the capital gain of others. We allow it to happen for the sake of superficial pleasures. In a commercial and superficial world, it would make sense to regard the idea of ageing as one that is taboo and terrible. Old age is construed as a life phase considered of no commercial value other than for selling dreams of past youth, or the quest for eternal youth; medication, **wait-until-you-die** homes and mobile vehicles. Some of these products and services provide a huge value to those in need of them, except the selling of dreams of past youth, or illusions of an eternal youth.

Is the ego of our youth and adulthood so large that becoming smaller as we age is seen as a downfall and not a progression?

What if ageing is a time for progressive change towards freedom from the chains of surviving superficial priorities that once seemed important? What if ageing meant that we could unstrap the wings of our souls to finally live a life ignited by a lighter purpose with deeper values for its limited duration?

The idea of buying more and more commodities that we never really need is a little harder to sell to an older demographic than to a younger, more naïve and unstable one. If the marketing of our lives is solely centred in demographics for money-making, then it may make sense to put the aged away. After all, it is a demographic that is possibly too experienced to easily buy into **The Noise** and a whole lot of crap!

In this environment, conscious wisdom is regarded as uncool and is encouraged to remain a commodity of low value. If ageing were to retrieve its original wealth in the status of wisdom, experience, serenity and the higher consciousness, it would not be an easy task in endeavouring to sell illusions.

Illusions to stay young forever, or illusions to achieve things one might never achieve would no longer hold the weight of valued importance to this older demographic. At some point, the illusion of an eternal life, which remains non-purchasable and non-negotiable, needs to be let go of in order to consciously design a life journey that leads to a celebrated grand finale.

What could happen if we were to bring 'sexy' back to being older? What if being older is thought of as the new 'cool' because sound reason and experience are to be celebrated and cherished? Such an attitude shift is guaranteed to keep us looking forwards, rather than backwards to what we once had, and who we once were. What if beyond the loud noise of the **Buy-Buy-Buy World** there is a sense of empowerment in the artistry of living a human life? A certain energetic and liberating feeling of consciousness would manifest itself, characterised by an age that brings back proactive wisdom, and restores balance in our lop-sided world.

What if the idea of old age were not perceived to be a burden based on conditions, such as healthcare? Instead, what if older persons were looked upon as mentors for living the best, healthy and purposeful lives? It is a useful demographic from which the next generations can learn. More importantly, older age is a time to try on a different intelligence that may not have had the possibility to surface before: an age of freedom from a self-created social normalcy that is full of weighted responsibilities, and has a tendency to last an entire lifetime. It is an age of power and possibility. A perfect time to ensure that a life lived consciously is never wasted or one full of regret.

We all grow older every day. This will remain a fact whether we choose to acknowledge it or not. As long as we connect with our consciousness and we are true to the life we are here to live, we will accumulate rich life experiences no matter the age. With the gift in growing older, such a person can only own a collection of stories worthy of being heard and revered. The wealth of such experiences cannot be put aside and quietened down. Instead, this wealth needs to shine in the forefront of civilisation as inspirational examples of wisdom, imperfections and joy in living for next generations of human beings.

It is a movement that is kinetic. It is accompanied by purposeful and grounding energy that is never stagnant. This is the energy of the 'New Old'.

A Side Story

On one of my travels I saw a TV ad. In the ad there was a woman in her late sixties. The ad was about funeral insurance. The woman goes about her daily routine and turns to the camera and says that she does not want her kids to pay for her funeral. This is why she will buy her own funeral insurance.

A question immediately popped up in my head: Did her kids pay for their birth? Rampant images and ideas such as this quietly portray that it is acceptable for our children and the younger generations to view our last phase in life as burdensome to them.

The birth of a new human being includes the complete and conscious involvement of at least one other human being, most naturally at least one of its parents or another loving and caring human being, for its care and development while it is still little and physically and mentally vulnerable.

Similarly, the last phase of life, including its death, cannot exclude the conscious involvement of a loving and caring human being connected to its life in relationship. This is a person or persons who will continue to be connected as they celebrate the drawing of a full-life circle of a life beautifully lived.

The Value of My Life

Who will decide the value of my life?
The one who gave birth to me?
The one who lifted me from trouble?
The one who tormented me with fear?
The one who respected me?
The one who beat me?
The one who loved me?
The one who taught me?
The one who hurt me?
The one who left me?
The one who used me?
The one who tortured me?
The one who called me "Mama"?
The one who celebrated me?
Only I will.
I will decide the value of my life.

Moving in the
Direction of
Persevered Action

We are never moving
or living away from
death.

We are always moving
towards death in
completing a natural
life-cycle.

This remains
a truth outside of the
noise of information
that surrounds us.

Childhood

- Controlled
- Contained
- Schooled
- Scheduled

Youth

- I am invincible
- I will be free
- I like what I like
- My friends
- My body

Childhood

- Free to be
- Learning
  - Connections
  - Self
  - Others
  - Nature
  - Life with death

Youth

- I am ready to design my life
- I am unique
- My skills, My crafts
- My travel as life
- My purpose in relation to others
- Respect of Self
- Respect of others
- I am of Service

Adult

- I make mistakes because I try to be better than I was yesterday
- My awareness
- How am I connected ?
- How do I give back ?
- My state of health
- Continous gratitude
- Dreams to real-time stories

Growing Older

Adult

My
* perfect job
* perfect man/woman
* perfect things
* perfect friends
* perfect house
* perfect life
* perfect family

* My duties
* My mortgage
* My wants

Senior

* My limitations
* My pain
* My loneliness
* My judgement
* My health
* My lost youth
* My frustrations
* My disappointments

Older

* My looming death
* My regrets
* What I did
* What I did not

Living Older

Senior

* My wrinkles
* My fading colors are in harmony
* My stories
* I am with life
* I am alive and of good use
* I am out of my comfort zone
* I know lots and I am still learning more
* Continuous gratitude
* I am with Awareness
* Wisdom
* Experiences converting to stories
* Soul freedom
* Strategic health

Older

* I am with love
* I am with community
* I am centred with Self
* I am in continous gratitude
* I am with life
* My living legacy
* Inspiration
* Freedom from attachments

6

Growing Older or Living Older?

Growing older and *Living Older* are not the same process. In the context of this book, here are the definitions:

Growing older is a way of being established by set behaviours that revolves continuously in the same way through the entirety of a life. This includes being an expert at repetitive and conditioned behaviour, even if it is of no service to Self and others. This way of being narrows down possibilities and options, often excluding an interest in the unknown. Such a way of living results in becoming and remaining a monolithic kind of creature throughout the journey of a beautiful living life, as if you were a king or queen of the comfort zone.

Imagery — Visualise a pool of water that has nowhere else to go but to stay within its predetermined perimeters.

Living Older is a way of being that requires practice and consciousness to cultivate a uniqueness of purpose through the entirety of a life. This includes all of the senses: seeing, smelling, hearing, tasting, touching, and understanding every situation, adventure and experience as if for the very first time, every time. This way of being allows the body, the mind and the emotions to relearn and re-evaluate each new situation with a sense of wonder and curiosity, equalling the magic of 'first times'. Living continuously in such a way throughout the multi-faceted experiences of our life journey is like being a king or queen of the thrill in uncertainty.

Imagery — Imagine the energy of a wild stream full of unknown and new possibilities as it finds a new path after an earthquake or an avalanche.

Living Older is a way of looking forwards instead of looking backwards. It adds a splash of awareness and sensuality by making us present for each transformation as it happens.

Taking a closer look at the negativity surrounding the ageing process, we can identify its origins as an old attitude. This narrow perception creates limitations, makes possibilities invisible and leaves us stripped of consciousness to be our authentic Self no matter our age.

We are often made to believe that the circle of life starts at birth, immediately followed by the necessary reasons for accumulating money, buying more things than we really need, remaining in a state of neediness and addiction, surviving if we can until we are no longer in the circle. This circle, by design, is very different from the original circle of life that has a starting point with birth and an ending point with death including the possibility to create whatever design we intend for all the valid phases in between.

Considerations in Living Older

- *Living Older* has nothing to do with actual chronological age.

- Wrinkled skin and grey hair are necessary physical manifestations for a healthy life transition. These changes may be an annoyance in our superficial world, much like the wearing of diapers may have been to us as babies. The signs of ageing serve as a reminder to question ourselves regarding the individually designed greatness that we have achieved as life is coming full circle.

- The excuses we make available to live our lives within safe limitations need to be replaced by the illumination of awareness in living our lives to the best of our individual purpose.

- Older age is not an excuse to alleviate the ugly traits of being human. If anything, it needs to be about beauty and about an accomplishment of the highest order.

- A position of honour is not automatically attained in being older, but it is earned from living a life full of experiences and the many stories lived.

- Everything that we may have done wrong has a time for correction. Perhaps 'the now' at any age is such a time.

- In *Living Older*, it is not a time to sit back and wait for death, or for the end of life, as we have known it. Instead, it is a time to live bigger and better than we have ever lived before.

- *Living Older* is designed for us to be full of allure and to be with a developed innate presence. It is powerful by design, and by will. Whether it is to hold a neighbour's hand, or to move mountains, *Living Older* has a personal weight and power to make any magic happen.

- *Living Older* is not a disease, or about disease. It is about a high level of care for Self and others.

- *Living Older* is about the awareness and acceptance of fluctuating limitations and strengths.

- *Living Older* is not an excuse for an unconscious life. It is not a legitimate excuse for failing to improve our Self at every level.

- *Living Older* is about not allowing our conscious Self to become a pawn in the game of marketing and advertising for products and services in a growing age of capitalism.

- *Living Older* does not think death. It thinks life.

- *Living Older* is not a time to stop dreaming. It is the time to pick up on those dreams that went astray, and to bring them back home again.

- *Living Older* does not have a predetermined START line created by marketing and advertising, or other limiting beliefs. Neither does it have a predetermined FINISH line created by marketing and advertising, or other limiting beliefs.

- *Living Older* is a time to add positivity into a vital transitory phase that is a part of living a beautiful life. In turn, this opens up doors through which opportunities can manifest themselves.

- *Living Older* is a time of true empowerment.

- *Living Older* is a time to learn to be free of attachments and belongings. The feeling of having nothing to lose becomes a lot more relevant.

Invariably, there will be many more considerations that become apparent when we turn our perceptions towards possibilities, rather than limitations. Living fully and consciously acknowledges that every unique phase in the journey of our lives is lived well and completely, as we naturally move forward in the revolving circle of life. In a marathon, the main objective is in completing the race. We celebrate the accomplishment of the completed race.

Why is it that ageing and finding our Self at the end of a great life cycle seems useless and uncelebrated?

A life is always waiting to be lived. The soul confirms its presence with every breath that we consciously take in to refresh its existence within our physical body. *Living Older* is in continuing to proceed into uncertainty. We should not worry about the capacities of our physical or mental states in the future. It is our responsibility to care for ourselves in the present. Our concern is not in waiting for our death. There is a good reason why we do not know when it will happen. *Living Older* is about learning and continuously evolving as human beings.

To experience the current perception of growing older, imagine that we are running our lives without consciousness as we speed through getting high on the earlier phases of life only to suddenly 'put the brakes on' because we are now older with less purpose as we wait near the FINISH line of life. *Living Older* gives us a lifetime, whatever the number, to live a meaningful life with the privilege to choose how we adorn it.

Living Older is not about the accumulation of money and the material comforts it provides. Money is as important as the right tool is to get a specific job done. The value it provides is temporary. *Living Older* is about the journey of living a life in all of its holistic consciousness. This serves us with a priceless and a soul-bearing value. *Living Older* requires that we continue to be brave. It takes a lot of courage to come out of an organised and comfortable life and into a life of newness and strangeness. Yet, this is what feeds our senses in order to remain alive with curiosity and adaptability in the uncertainty of life.

So when does any kind of old happen? The answer is subjective to the individual person. Some people have been old since they were twenty, or even younger. Unlike physical decline, an attitude has no visible signs of ageing.

I have understood the need to prepare for growing older. I recommend you begin the day you realise that it is time to invest in *Living Older*. Preparation can be facilitated if you are able to look at natural death straight in the eye. For those of us who cannot give up on their youth and their unfulfilled past, preparation will prove to be more of a challenge.

Growing older is a journey that moves further into being more and more old. *Living Older*, on the other hand, is living in the new moment many times over, until the physical journey ends. By achieving the quality of living with gusto and oomph in *Living Older*, we will experience fewer yearnings to put this vibrant circle of life in reverse gear.

What became of our need for the elders, the wisdom holders and the sages? These are not just older people. They are people who have lived, and even after they are gone, they will continue to live in the continuity of the circle of life.

This book is written with the intention of introducing some simple, some strange, some radical, and some silly concepts to the idea of *Living Older*. After all, what can we expect from an environment of radical change?

If the effort put into trying to reverse ageing were converted to the effort spent in enriching the art of living a beautiful life, we would all be laughing our way to The Finale.

We can either envision growing older to be a progressive state that brings us closer to death, or we can envision *Living Older* as a body that progressively serves its limited time while the soul resides in it, enlarging every single day as it gathers the best experiences in being alive.

Like the glass half full or the glass half empty analogy, the quality in *Living Older* is a matter of attitude and choice.

An Ignorant Comparison

We often make comparisons between an older person and a younger person. This usually takes place with a set of criteria that favours a younger person. For example, as is often portrayed by the media, the younger person's strengths or abilities are contrasted with the apparent weaknesses of the older person.

When asked to draw an image of 'old', we add a stick, a hunched back and a sense of heightened uselessness. Comparisons are based on the generalised standards set out by messages delivered repeatedly every day. We follow up by setting our standards accordingly, including how we spend our money, what we choose to surround ourselves with, and how we create our ways of being.

The definition we give to the meaning of life today is often one-sided, with the spotlight on being young. We give in to every whim of childhood, lest our youth feel deprived. We accord an utmost glorification to the idea of youth; we worship money and its illusions while in our thirties and forties, and then we abruptly close down with a hush when growing older. Ideally, we need each phase in the sacred circle of life to connect to the one before it, as it complements in purpose and unique importance, rather than competing, with the egos of each vital stage in our lives.

We commence our battles against ageing by using the word 'anti', and we simultaneously shut down our abilities to be 'pro' ageing. We can start to create better and more realistic opportunities to illuminate the many advantages that come with being an older person. Examples could be in curating the wealth of stories about mistakes and imperfections that accumulate with age. Or in the design of wrinkles casting a permanent smile on the face that becomes a representation for a life well lived with no aura of regret.

Life is a beautifully complex experience that is unique for every human being at each different moment of its journey. When it is subjected to comparisons and competition, there is no beneficial gain for the individual life; there is only strife.

What If

What if
all this time
it has been
useful for some
to keep
the wisdom and
the consciousness
of the elders numb,
quiet and
uselessly succumbed.
So that the
loud noise
of unconscious
trading and deeds
that keep the rest of us
wanting
more and more and more
succeeds.
While the earth
we live in
slowly dies,
the noise continues to ring loud
and quietly hum
to keep our
living
consciousness
dumb?

Ask Not How Old I Am. Ask How I Have Lived My Life!

I will look as I have lived.
Free to live. Many Oh! Many stories in the folds of my face.
Wisdom in the fading colours of my hair.

7

Life Before
I Wanted to
Live Older

My love of life stemmed from the many distinctive circumstances that came my way. It was a trend that continued to provide me with life experiences I felt were right by intuition, pushing me into unknown and uncomfortable situations, rather than leaving me to wait in more familiar surroundings as life happened to me. These collective experiences brought about an exceptional blend of colours which were used to paint the canvas of my first fifty some years. These became permanent traits that led me naturally towards a conscious passion in *Living Older*.

I was born into a family that I believed to be a mismatch, the kind that keeps you wondering, 'Really? Why do I not look like my family? Why do I not think like my family?' It is the kind of family that reminds you of being in a movie where you are the main character and everyone else is speaking in a language you do not understand. In due time, I understood that they were all normal. I was the one who was different.

I am not a natural follower. No matter how much people around me wanted me to do what was considered acceptable, I could not conform if I did not truly believe in its purpose. This is not to say that I think I am better or worse than anyone else.

When we are in contact with the unique essence of who we are, we see fewer differences and more similarities in the people around us. This realisation opens up a wide world of opportunities for love, peace and deep understanding.

I could always see a path that was not easily visible to many around me. There was always a way. Often it was a distinctively different path from the crowd, but I was aware that it was always there, covered in the most extraordinary and useful 'weeds' that served me.

By the time I was thirty-eight, I had been working and playing in my favourite industry of hotels and restaurants for twenty years. But the monotonous spiral of continuity in a limited space became more and more evident. My soul was yearning to experience something simpler, but of a larger purpose. I conversed with the Universe and asked to be of meaningful service—to be a part of something more important than day after day wheeling and dealing.

Less than a year later, I became pregnant with my beautiful daughter, thirteen years after having my beautiful son. Four months after she was born, my gynaecologist told me that I had cancer. He also told me that at the rate it was spreading, I had not much time to live. I had asked the Universe for my purpose, but instead I was being told that I was at 'the exit door'.

A sense of calm Zen with immense depth and power became my companion as I ventured forth into the next chapter in the journey of my life with fearlessness, focus, love, and passion. Together, all of these drives taught me a better understanding of my deeper Self. They provided for me strength and a power to accept what was willed to be. Thirteen years later, I am living with a new truth. My journey has been about living with purpose every single day. I have not accomplished many great feats; however, just smiling at the moon in recognition that it was there was considered purposeful enough for me!

My stories are large and beautiful. They are full of interesting imperfections. They are not grandiose according to any fixed template, but they are stories that have done me proud. They allow me to lift my head up high with pride for having lived my life in its unique blend of colours.

An adventurous life is painted with many colours, including some dark shades in its composition. There are hardships and difficulties, but also opportunities to make choices at transitional stages on my life journey. I revel in the quiet glories of my life, my private celebrations in knowing that life is indeed beautiful. I have not found any reason to believe that it will be any different moving forward, as the chapters of my remaining life unfold.

If anything, I sense that the experience in living my life adventurously has added a deep power to my core. Having lived such a celebrated life, I am convinced that life's beauty will continue to grow while my body starts to change. As a living entity, I am of life and I have choices just like every other person who is alive.

It is time to come out of the conscious numbness. There is no room for excuses in *Living Older*. No excuses.

There is truth in the expression, 'You only live once,' but the 'once' does not stop until the last breath has left us.

8

On My Way to a Life of Learning to Live Older

Life is big when you are connected to a purpose, and years have the ability to pass very quickly. I have found it necessary to create a list of reminders, guidelines and checklists to help me remember what I need in my new pursuit and practice of *Living Older*.

It was obvious to me that there was no existing word that could best describe this collection of guidelines. I shared my difficulty in finding the ideal expression with my young daughter, who was eleven at the time. After only a few minutes, she suggested, in a very matter of fact way, that I use the word **evolver**. As soon as I heard her speak, all of my thoughts and senses fell upon the suggested word, just like you would settle on a very comfortable couch full of fluffy cushions!

The word evolver is not an officially recognised word in most dictionaries but it could be considered to be a noun for someone who is evolving. It is an apt word to use for guiding principles that are continuous, of which the designs and outcomes will be different for each individual who will choose to give them some thought as they begin to practice them.

Allow me to present to you 55 evolvers that I have adopted, which will assist you in your travels in *Living Older*. I will add to this list, as my journey gets deeper and deeper. These evolvers represent a thought process of simple ways of being you can adopt, adapt, dance with, comment on, criticise, or put in the washing machine and hang out to dry!

What each one of us does with the evolvers is subject to who we are as individuals, or who we intend to be or not to be. The evolvers in this book are not listed according to any priority or importance. Every different person will respond to or adopt each evolver according to what their needs will determine. They are not criteria for evoking competition. Certainly, they are not perfect or idealistic. They are available much like paints of many different colours and textures are available—to assist you in creating the unique painting which is your life.

Just like any human being, I have a tendency to stray a little off course.

The evolvers provide a foundational reminder for me, helping me to get back on the conscious path of living whenever I stray. They lead me back like a true North does on the compass. I hope they will assist you too, dear reader, as you take baby steps into the uncertainties of your increasing years. Use the evolvers as a guide to create your own shades of colours and light in choosing to *Live Older.*

The Game of Living Older

1. Feel Alive
* What keeps you alive?
* Where is your newness?
* Are you vulnerable?

2. Health
* Who owns yours?
* A pro-health lifestyle or a con-health lifestyle?
* Seek the company of Awareness.
* Are you grounded?
* Are you connected to your core?

3. Purpose
* Creative Flow or Stagnant Creativity?
* Is yours tied to a job?
* What is the value of your life to another living person?

4. Habits
* Preventive, Defensive or Reconstructive?
* Maintain and keep those that serve you. Discard and detach from those that do not serve you.
* Practice new ones to serve your Now.
* Make the necessary mistakes.

5. Pleasure
* Play with your senses.
* Create reasons to acquire and to use pleasure daily.
* Enjoy 'Alone' time with Self.
* Be of service to others.

6. Relationships
* Do you require a partner or a needy attachment?
* Are you losing Self in the partnership?
* Is there space to be 'You' as an individual?
* Is there a balance of mutual agreements and values?

7. Pass It On
* Inspire just one person at a time.
* What priceless gift are you leaving behind?

8. Turn-On Wisdom
* Befriend consciousness.
* Silence is communication.
* Know when to keep quiet.

9. Celebrations
* Not just birthdays.
* Create mini reasons to celebrate very often.
* Develop courage to be 'weird'.

10. To Slave or not to Slave
* Be true to your purpose and to your values.
* Learn to be in business for your Self.
* Money as a tool to do what you need to do, or money as the core of your life?

11. A Designer Lifestyle
* No outsourcing
* Own your life.
* Stay with consciousness, not with confusion especially in times of trouble.
* Are you seeking a perfection of some kind?

12. Work with Nature
* Are you connected to something bigger than this Earth?
* Are you invincible?
* Fear of death - Why?

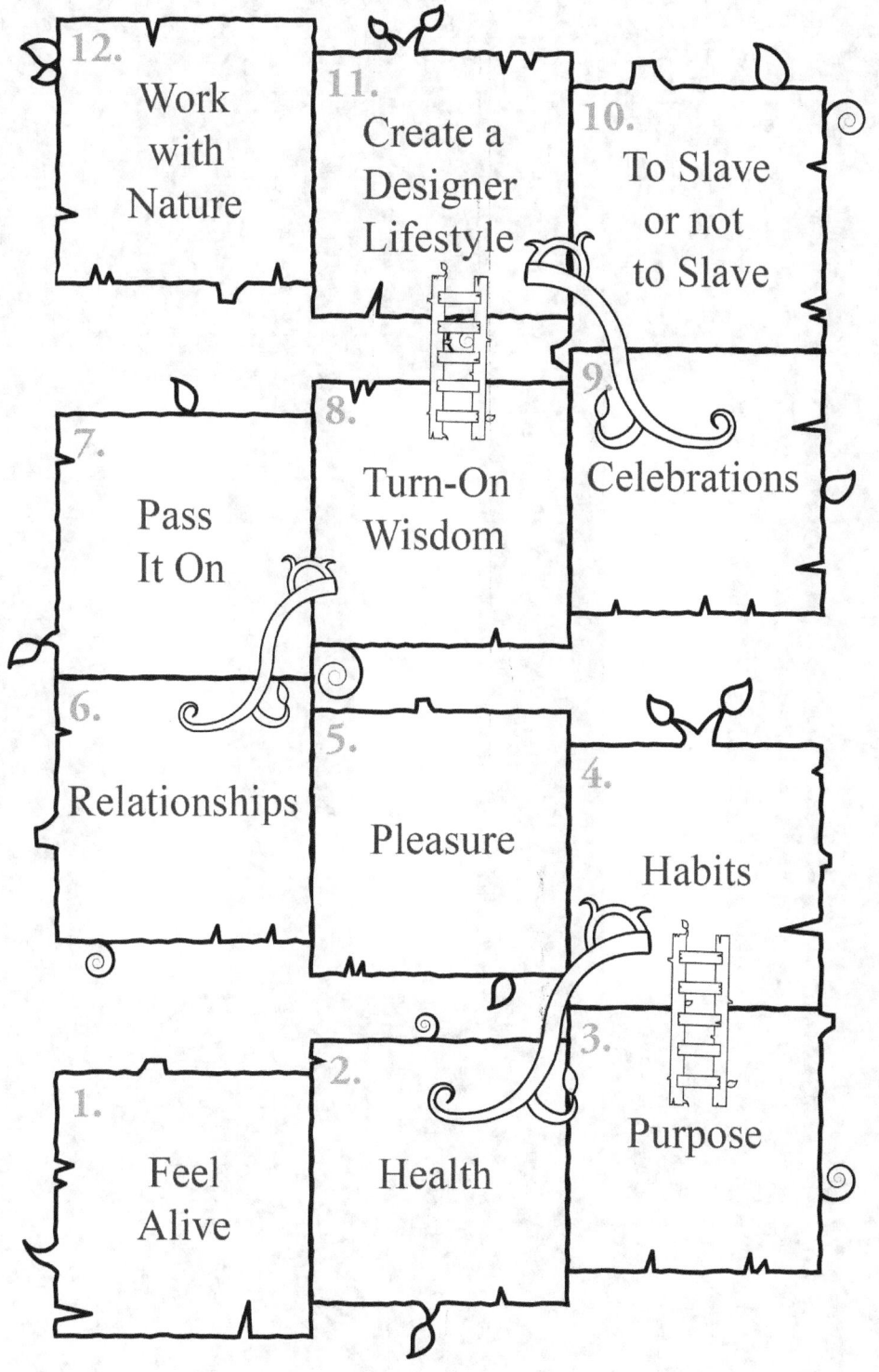

Evolvers for Inspiration and Practice

9

55 Evolvers for Living Older

You will find that some of the evolvers are easy to adopt and to practice. Others may be difficult to assimilate or may not offer you a connection to your unique life. Some of the evolvers are familiar to you and others may be considered new. These are not gems of expertise you can collect or bottle for sale. Instead, they are ideas for a lifetime of practice, with different outcomes for different types of beautifully unique humans.

You may discover that even a slight degree of difference matters in an evolver's unique qualities and its value for inspiration. The outcome will vary depending on the different energies surrounding you at any given moment. The evolvers are certainly connected to each other, very much as we are to each other. Many can be practiced in combination or as an aggregate.

To ignite the magic that they hold, each evolver needs to be acknowledged by committing it to conscious practice. I suggest you allow for a lifetime of fun, learning and experimentation as you try the evolvers on for size, and I hope, you too will learn to fall in love with *Living Older*.

Because the 55 Evolvers are created from holistic attributes, for ease of reference, they are loosely categorised as one of the following:

1. The Attitude
2. The Mental
3. The Environment
4. The Spirit
5. The Emotional
6. The Physical

Keep in Mind

There are many possibilities within each evolver. The book serves as a preparatory platform to introduce the evolvers within a concept of *Living Older* instead of growing older. Unique individuals and extraordinary groups of people who are looking to benefit from acquiring a more accurate understanding of WOWAGEING™ and The Art of Living Older as well as how to follow a deeper and a more guided practice of the 55 evolvers are invited to wowageing.com to explore more information concerning events, workshops, courses, travel and gatherings which will be organised worldwide on a regular basis.

The Attitude

*I see same things
different.
I see different things
same.
It took me time
to get your game.
My smile,
My shiny eyes,
My wild soul,
confused
as you played.
But now
I know
your strength,
your beauty.
My smile,
My shiny eyes,
My wild soul,
aroused.
Curious.
What will you bring?
As I journey now
Stronger
than ever before.
What will we create?*

1.
Be The Rock Star Of Your Own Kingdom

There is something mesmerising about rock stars, pop stars or movie stars who can take away our entire attention with no allowance for logical interruption.

However, when the alluring veil is lifted and we are able to focus our intellectual minds towards this phenomenon with a deeper reflection, we find there are some obvious reasons for this out-of-control attraction that stand out. First, we are always looking 'up' to them. Secondly, they entertain us. Entertainment wins over work anytime! Thirdly, in their presence, we forget our worries and uncertainty. Finally, we watch, admire or critique what someone else is doing, a practice which is always a lot more fun than critiquing the Self.

Before a rock star earns the title, they need to have the ability to entertain us. They need to be high on passion. They need to know how they are going to magnetise and mesmerise us. Is it in their look, their charisma? Some of the criteria for superficial attraction are obvious. We can argue that not all ordained rock stars are actually talented; rather, it is their special magic in combining the many elements that gets us. Who these people are off-stage as human beings is dependent on how they live their lives just as much as any one of us, but what remains of vital importance is that on stage they own their represented space. This energy is what magnetises us.

I always believed I was a rock star even before I realised I owned the Kingdom of my Life.

The concept of this belief fit 'my every pore'. It did not matter that I do not play a musical instrument. It only mattered that I felt every bit of this energy's passionate vibe. No one else needed to acknowledge the right solely owned by me and no one could take this away from me. The accompanying freedom was earned in knowing what I felt was not attached to a requirement in being accepted by others or in owning a sizeable fan club.

Every human being has the right to dream dreams that are as far fetched as we can possibly dream them, or as simple and accountable as we can create them. A dream remains an idea when there is no action to accompany it. Ideas are necessary, but they come and they disappear very quickly, much like cloud formations. Cloud shapes move and constantly shift before they disappear. When we are in sync with our dreams, we have the ability to turn them into reality by adding the vital step of action. This is where the magnetic energy lies in turning a dream into a real possibility. The practice cannot be bottled as a commodity and sold for money. It needs you to repeatedly commit to doing the work for the magnetic magic to be created.

The nature in assuring its success, unfortunately, requires more than just having the dream before working towards acting on it. 'Owning the dream' is a necessity. Owning a stable space to create the dream is vital. If we do not own it, the dream does not have the strength and ability to convert into a physical or visual entity that now has the priceless value in being a true reality.

A big challenge in the ownership of an individual's dream within our global world today is the constant noise of disapproval and the comfortable cushioning from mistakes, both of which are available as easy, ready-made choices in keeping us within the narrow approval system of a larger body or herd—in **sheep language** such as, 'What is someone else going to think about my dream or idea'? 'What if they do not like it'? 'What if I stand out'? This list will continue to grow with a whole lot more **What-if-ers**?

For many of us, the high-speed, global world of the Internet that we have created, applauded and brought into our lives, is closer to us than our innate higher consciousness. The speed in access has helped us to magnify our material dreams to exponential levels. On the darker side; however, we have allowed the high-speed world of the Internet to enter and to fill up the unique private spaces inside of our heads and in many of our cells, allowing them to 'dance' to a myriad of emotions driven by a vast reception of information to a tune that is orchestrated by everything other than the owner of the Self.

Ultrafast and convenient communication has brought along with it some very dangerous messages encrypted within this noise—messages that are not readily apparent as threatening. Ostensibly, these messages actually seem caring and concerning. In reality, they are engineered for the benefit and for the profit of someone other than the true Self. The ability to lose our Self starts to get easier and easier when these malicious messages sneak into our private head space during a vulnerable moment in the journey of our life, inviting us to be entertained, often unconsciously. As these disguised messages are designed for entertainment to our senses, we proceed, unknowingly, to give away our rights and our dignity to them. We allow them to tell us who we are and who we need to be as well as what we need to like and what we need to dislike.

We easily become what others want us to become.

Our ever-ready desire for acceptance and our unconscious, numbed minds welcome these messages that tell us being old is an 'anti' thing. They enforce the notion that being sick is a natural part of growing older and they make allowances for us to believe that being burdensome is a natural side-effect in growing older. Considering the many years of experience, these messages have grown in power and continue to do so. After all, it is an easy feat to achieve when our consciousness is made numb or when it is branded as unworthy—something to be screened out of our very busy lives.

What replaces our 'switched off' consciousness is an emptiness we readily fill up with soothing messages from outside. Numb and needy are very easy states to be in the world of today.

We become a victim by design of what others limit us to believe.

If the world is highly dis-eased today, is it likely that we have yet to find workable solutions as change-makers because we are not in touch with our individuality?

Is it possible within the ordinary state of our being that there are hidden, untapped superpowers?

So, who decided there were only limited ways to becoming a rock star?

The way we parent, lead, create, learn or live depends on who we are as human beings. It is not in what we wear, not because of our sexual or religious preferences, not in how much money we have or earn, not because of gender or age, and not even due to the environment or conditioning of our upbringing. These are only decorations we use to adorn ourselves during the journey of our lives, like buying souvenirs from a trip. If this concept rings true, we can remove what we no longer need to wear, like souvenirs that lose their nostalgic value upon returning to real life.

Who I am, if recognised, acknowledged and accepted by my Self is much more profound than what I choose to wear seasonally. When my focus is on what I do not have in comparison to others, I lose track of the time required to build my stage firmly on the uniqueness that is mine and mine alone. Standing firm in support of who we are as unique individuals capable of love and contribution is truly mesmerising. In taking ownership of our presence, all of us can achieve some small but important success in just being the best of our true beings.

Mother Theresa is a legend. She was a 'rock star' of her own kingdom. There are many other people on this planet who accomplish some extraordinary feats for the betterment of human kind. They may not be in the theatres or filling up stadiums to entertain us, but they do profoundly rock the stage of humanity. We can still hear them although there is no sound. We can hear and feel the deep vibrations of their deeds whether we are listening or not.

Ownership and embodiment of the Self are foundational requirements in *Living Older* for it requires that we own the life we are given before we can seek to live it fully as a true Self. If I do not own my stage, how can I be a rock star? Your stage is yours. If you do not see it, it is because you have not built it yet.

Build it.

As long as you are breathing, there is no such thing as it being too late, unless you are limited by your own beliefs. When you are aligned to the true North of your individual purpose, the entertainment will begin. The people who need you will come and the inspired crowd will cheer. The crowd may not be present in big numbers since it is not about math or money. The crowd may simply be someone you have touched and inspired, or whose feathers you dared to ruffle so as to initiate a positive change in their Self.

If I am down to just one such person in the audience for the performance of my life, my status of rock star in my own kingdom will be a roaring success!

A Side Story

There have been numerous occasions in my life when being different or not complying with a larger number of people has been questioned. The youngest of five girls, I was considered 'un-girly' because I did not care for makeup and other such interests. Instead, I made sports my high. Makeup just did not have a logical purpose in my thrill for sport. The exhilaration in sport brought to me a need to better myself while working to understand the 'un-limitations' of my physical body in play, as well as in understanding the limits of my growing ego amidst a team.

My liberated feet have always felt highly comfortable in sports shoes. A strong penchant for sneakers started when I was thirteen. Since then, I began a collection of the strangest designs that decorated my feet as if I were dressing for a carnival. My choice of highly decorative shoes remained a constant as my soul grew to love walking—my favourite mode of transport. I even found flair by wearing my shoes with gowns and at dress-up events. Of course, this always attracted plenty of looks of both fascination and disapproval. Yet, not once did a questioning look deter me. How could it? It was I who felt immense freedom walking in my own shoes!

My Expression in Style

I love for the clothes I wear to express my many different moods and states of being. They entertain and inspire me into the role I am playing at any given day of my life. Any limitation or standard in its regard has nothing to do with the script in my head and everything to do with the script of someone else's chosen life path. My self-expression in clothes is sheer window-dressing entertainment created primarily for my own pleasure.

My Love for Many Types of Work

After graduating from hotel school and entering the real world of work and money, I got bored very quickly. I was not impressed by titles, nor was I interested in ladders that everyone was queuing up to wear or to climb. I chose to remove myself from large businesses and began immersing myself in many other experiences that led the way to different types of work. Today, the many skills I have attained enable me to switch from one type of work to another according to what is in demand for the exchange of supply.

In creating my life experiences, what matters to me is what I do. It does not matter to me that the majority are doing this or they are doing that. This allows me time to make the mistakes I need to make and to enjoy the makings of my personal life journey. Insecurities are recurring with the same waves that I ride for change. No matter the challenges I face, there is a resolution—if not for good, then for the time required in moving on. 'Did I do the best that I could?' 'Did I design my life the way my residing soul intended?' Questions like these are never-ending, coming at me like splashes of water that cannot be avoided when surfing my life journey. In discipline, every unimportant sound becomes background noise in the environment of my modern day life.

I can consciously remove The Noise, or I can keep it playing as it takes root in my being. All we need is to create a consciousness button like a volume/mute button on our tech devices and use it to silence this noise or play it loud. The choice is ours.

This evolver is not limited to a unique talent or a lucky blessing bestowed upon me. It is a matter of choice that comes with undeterred practice due to its difficult nature. It is a choice that must be made by the Self. The sweet reward of its aftermath comes in the form of joyous rays of a deep smile felt in the depths of your core.

Your Rock Star Kingdom

Create it

Start by taking inventory of who you really are.

Ask yourself, 'Who am I?' A question to ask repeatedly at any given time when evolving constantly. Herein, lies the magic trick. The answer to knowing 'who I am' is not meant to be clear in its wisdom or to represent a certainty that will never shift in a lifetime. The question is much easier to evaluate when you have lived a life of significant opportunities, experiences and stories that provide a certification in the nature of 'who I am' and 'who I can be'.

Create a filter system for information and communication.

Allow in your kingdom only what you choose to listen to. Cut off any verbal or written noise that you do not need in your kingdom. Everyone can say what one wants to say; it is only up to you and you alone to listen or to hear it. This tool will help you to come back into focus and to the centre of who you are.

Cultivate a culture of love, respect and freedom.

Your individual kingdom is designed for you. Its freedom depends on your respect for other individual kingdoms that are designed to their own unique specifications. Remember not all rock star kingdoms look the same because we are all designers using the creativity of our own life experiences as a blueprint. We are, however, naturally compelled to inspire and to be inspired by some kingdoms that are worthy of our admiration.

Create invitations for other 'life designers' to experience & celebrate your way of life.

Share ideas and ways of being that you adopt into your kingdom or abolish from your kingdom. practice of choosing and sharing that is done compassionately without hurting anyone in the process.

Blame no one else.

There is no one to blame in your kingdom. Mistakes are allowed because you will want to venture out into ways of thinking that are not as yet in existence. There is no one to inhibit you or to control your individual life apart from the Self.

Stop controlling a life of another.

There is no need to control anyone in your kingdom. The only control in effect is to remember that your freedom stays within your own kingdom and that there are rules to respect when visiting the space of other kingdoms.

Introduce plenty of rhythm into the kingdom.

There is a natural vibe that rocks your world daily. Its rhythm is created as a result of contentment in knowing your limitations, weaknesses and strengths. There is a joy in understanding that you are not perfect and that you are designed with the skill in adaptability to many changes in and around you. Cherish knowing there are valuable lessons to learn every new day, perhaps in every new moment.

You are the creator of your own obstructions, limitations and high standards.

There may be times when unkind words from another cause you to 'trip' on what you believe to be true. At times like this, there is no longer a need to pretend that you will not fall. Instead, know to be true that you can get up from the fall and every time you get up from a fall, you will be reinforced with more confidence in the choice of life that is your kingdom.

Create a purpose to be of service.

Your kingdom will have no purpose if it does not serve another kingdom in any form of variable exchanges. It is up to you to find your audience, to entertain them with connection, and to mesmerise them into being the best in their respective kingdoms.

There is only one life.

It is up to you how you live it. What you make of the abundance or the lack of materials provided to you in building your kingdom is exactly where the magic in your life resides.

2.
Looking
Good.
According
To Whom?

Who would win if all the fish and mammals in the ocean were to decide which creature was the most beautiful of them all?

What categories would they need to use? How would a justifiable comparison take place? Apart from our obvious lack of fins and gills, how are we as human beings different?

Human beings have amazing abilities but are unintelligent when it comes to basic behaviours. The physical look we acquire is either ours by inheritance or we can consider it to be random selection, if need be. Love it or hate it, whichever sentiment we adopt, it remains ours. How we feel about our physical look does not provide us with a justification or an authority to create a template that is forced upon another for compliance.

Before we go too far into feelings about our physical Self, let us ask some questions, 'Where do we receive these "invisible" guidelines against how we measure ourselves'? 'Why is the spotlight on our looks'? When we consider the opinions of others, we allow them access to our power—the superpower of our life. Take for an example, a king or queen of an empire who allows another ruler and his people to come into their territory, providing them with access to their personal space for whatever the 'outsiders' want to do with it, regardless of their differences. No such leader in their complete awareness would make such a decision.

Our wish to look good fulfils a basic, natural requirement designed by Nature—an innate, primitive requirement that needs for us to be accepted by another. There is nothing wrong with that, except when approval is dependent solely on what another has set out as a singular standard in looking good.

Introduce confidence. How much confidence do we have right now? Its availability is not dependent on a currency or a monetary value. You are not able to buy it in retail, wholesale or even online. Where did yours go? Only you can find it because it never left you. It is reluctantly kept numbed against its will, waiting to be released by you. Before it takes its rightful place in the design of your life, you first need to affirm what your physical identity is to your Self, and how important it is what another will think of it.

Look in the mirror. Notice if you cringe at the reflection. Notice whether another person's image appears as an automatic comparison, perhaps even a younger Self. Notice, as well, whether you disassemble your body into bits and pieces to trade for the highest compliment; whether you compare yourself to an unrealistic image; whether you spend too much time at the mirror.

Consider if the constant comparisons are causing your authentic presence to be unstable on the shaky ground you have provided for it. Consider, too, if this is resulting in you spending less time creating beauty with your unique Self. The simplest truth that is very difficult to keep on firm ground is that there is only one original version of us. In a collector's world, this is considered priceless.

I am the only me there is.

This is a reason enough to be confident. The only legitimate comparison to consider is whether I am better than I was before or worse than I have been, as I remain present in my life journey. When we are accepting of our own standards for our description in looking good, we accept that our physical appearance cannot be appealing to everyone. This would be like forcing everyone to like every colour or every food on the planet.

In the restaurant business, the faster I learned that I could not please all our customers, the quicker I succeeded. On the stage where you play a unique life story, what does the choreography of your dance look like? Are you designing it on a loose foundation of the whims of others, or do you take control of its creation to appease your soul's needs? Your exclusive life experience, witnessed even by only one other person who counts, will remain an imprint long after you are gone.

Such silly people we are who place a huge weight of importance to a physical body that is eventually left behind to feed other life forms in the complete journey of a life well-lived.

Who decided that older people were to look a certain way? Who decided that creativity in style was limited to being young, whatever the interpretation of being young means? I am not implying that people who choose to adopt a quieter look are wrong or that they need to be deemed old. I am suggesting that creativity is ageless and that having fun in creative ways of expressing ourselves is not limited to an age. It is a playful game available to any person who is 'alive' and connected to their soul. Perhaps you will, slowly but surely, begin to notice that there is a wealth of traits available to delight you with human behaviour beyond another's opinion on how good you look superficially.

In *Living Older,* take the courage to play with style. Explore places and activities where you have never gone before. As long as you remain in a healthy, legal parameter, there is a vast space for play with style.

If what you want does not exist, it is your time to design it. Vive la différence!

Wear your individuality with fun and walk it proud.

Look
Good for
Your Self

A Sprinkle of Suggestions

A wild soul celebrates individuality. Its groove is like musical masterpieces that, although appreciated for their individual greatness, are lauded for their accompaniment to other instruments in creating awesome sounds.

Let your eyes sparkle with curiosity.

Allow your wild soul to dance to an inner groove that only you can hear.

Release your smile to open up a smile on someone else's face. Connect with the contagious energy!

Wear the many shades of grey on your head like the crown of wisdom it deserves. The definition of wisdom is a private one only you can share in your stories.

Seek to be outside of a self-imposed comfort zone. Feel the rush of adrenaline, from doing something different, which will make your skin glow.

Use all of your senses in what you set out to create.

Make something from your heart, with your hands, for someone else.

Look Good for Your Self

A Practice

Listen to the voices that determine your standards on Self.

If the voices belong to someone else, investigate consciously who let them in and why they were allowed into your Self. If you no longer need these voices, visualise a little trash bin at the end of your mind. Drag the messages in and dispense of them. For a more dramatic effect, put their invisible but heavy weight into the toilet bowl and flush them. Be very quick about it.

If the voices are your own, ask yourself if this recorded message is still serving you. If it is not, erase it and record a new one in its place.

Now dress your Self up to the way you and only you want to be, and take your accepted Self out on a parade for a people watching celebration.

The next time you have the urge to criticise someone else, start humming an 80's tune and move your head in its rhythm. The urge to criticise another will leave you very quickly in a big fright.

Living Older Looking Good

An Exercise in Imagery

1. Close your eyes.

2. Visualise yourself. Bear in mind that this vision is not necessarily a real picture of your Self. Create a vision of how you perceive your Self in your mind.

3. If the vision is blurred, sharpen it by filling in the blurred areas. What are these blurred lines? Why can you not see a sharper vision of your Self? In creativity, even your eyesight has no excuses. Do you see and hear laughter, noise, colour, or a variety in style of clothes, hair and makeup? Proceed when you are better able to see a sharper vision of your Self.

4. Inhale a deep, slow and conscious breath as you keep this image in your vision.

5. Exhale a deep, slow and conscious breath as you remove every negative sound, thought and word that may have come your way.

6. Keep your eyes closed. Imagine a vision of your Self one more time.

7. What do you see and hear? Paleness? A uniformed look? A certain haircut or hair-style that is no longer serving you as a piece of art?

8. In keeping with the respect for your unique individuality, add any creative colour, design and any special effect to your vision. Practice not using an example of another person to draw on your creativity. Use the powerful creativity of your own uniqueness.

9. Practice one to eight times according to the need in the moment.

10. Stay here for as long as you need, and come back here as often as you would like to come.

11. Open your eyes.

12. Go live the design of your life.

Living Older
Looking Good

Beautiful and Expressive Ideas

1. If you are losing hair prematurely or if your hair has weakened, take the opportunity to create an art form out of it. Shave your head and paint it using natural products. Convert it to a creative canvas for expression that can change as often as you would like it to change.

2. Wear wrinkles like a canvas of explicit artistry.

3. Choose to wear clothes that are theatrical. They are designed to tell stories. The experience of your presence on Earth is in your favour in accordance with your unique allure.

4. Wear shoes that are designed for great comfort but are creative art showpieces of expression.

Try these ides on for fun, I know I will!

3.
Blame
No One
For Where
You Are
Today

Living a life is so full of contradictions. We know how to be good. Yet, being bad is so much easier.

Very often, we know what we need to do but it is easier to pretend not to know it. As the years in living a life begin to add up, the stories increase, depending on the flavours that have been added in the cooking of our experiences. The beauty, in this art we call living a life, must include some bitter tasting events among the many better tasting ones. Mostly, the diversity in outcomes is essential to achieving the most awesome tasting experiences. Yet, when we get too attached to selecting the better tasting ones as our prime choice, we lose the ability to achieve the extraordinary.

One easy way to avoid looking inwards at the foundations of our own life design is by connecting the cause of a problem affecting Self to someone else. This tool is, by definition, commonly identified as 'blame'. Here is my definition of blame: an effective method to relieve oneself of immediate ownership of a problem, especially one directly related to the design in development of a Self.

Blame is such an easy concept to adopt. If it is someone else who is carrying it, then it does not concern us, it concerns someone else. In the course of a lifetime, we will have made some serious, and some not so serious, mistakes. The missing ingredient in the theatrical play of mistakes is ownership. If we have not considered the concept of owning our mistakes as yet, it is time we do. At the same time, let other people off the 'blame hook', the hook on which we have held them through our current lifetime.

In my many relationships with people, I have been a part of outcomes that hurt me or I have been in situations that have caused another person pain due to my actions. I made a personal choice to release myself from the clutches of blame. It is not an easy exercise to practice when you are bearing the painful consequences of your actions. The difficulty in its practice is no competition for the vibrant lightness of being that soon takes over as a side-effect of adopting a stand on the ownership of Self. The baggage of blame we carry throughout our lives creates a false protection, which provides ecstatic relief and pleasure temporarily. This is quickly replaced by a long-term pain in the back from the burden of carrying **blame baggage.**

To elaborate, we can agree that the responsibility of consequences in our child -hood is an important bearer on our physical Self. These were circumstances beyond our control at a time when we were helpless and dependent on our parents or caregivers, and our environment for nurturing us. When this time in our lives does not go well, we may choose to blame our parents for who we are, or for who we are not, as a result of their bad decisions.

The choice in blaming someone else provides us with the opportunity to excuse ourselves for not shifting our 'wronged selves' onto a path that would suit our 'right selves'. Blaming allows us to point the finger away from us. This visually looks good because the bad attention is taken away from us; however, it leaves us carrying a heavier, invisible baggage on our shoulders. Blame provides a free pass to avoiding the difficult path of self-change and self-redirection. The ironic side-effect of this decision is that our own life becomes one that is limited and burdened. It is only upon involving our conscious wild soul that we may discover the burden is easy to discard.

Discarding blame proves to be a vital strategy in gaining a well-lived life. If you choose to carry this baggage, on the other hand, be aware that as years add onto the path of your life journey, your shoulders will feel heavier physically as they begin to hunch forward with its weighted energy. Your soul may lose its lightness, and its larger need to be open and curious could be crushed by the weight of blame.

In *Living Older*, we begin to understand that like a good story, a good life needs all kinds of flavours, challenges and edges. If we are wronged in a chosen or unwanted relationship, we will mourn, pick ourselves up, dust our knees, taste the pain, and remember how good it is to be alive.

We forgive. We forgive so that we become unstuck from the quicksand of the weight of blame and we continue living the stories of our fascinating and unique lives.

We forgive because we have the mighty ability to do so.

The Backpack of Blame and the 100KM Hike

What The 'Backpack of Blame' and the 100km hike

When Anytime you feel the heavy weight of blame

Where Anywhere

Why Understand that carrying blame is heavy and unnecessary

1. Get a backpack. Pick a size that suits your needs for a 100km hike.

2. Fill up the backpack with unnecessary items until it is completely packed with weight.

3. Prepare Self for a 100km hike. Include planning a route that equals a 100km.

4. Put the backpack on and start walking.

5. Try your best to enjoy the walk.

6. Be conscious of the weight of the unnecessary backpack you are carrying.

7. Feel your body begin to complain.

8. Feel your joyful mood begin to waiver.

9. Be conscious of the stupidity in carrying such a large pack full of stuff you do not need that is weighing you down.

10. Alternatively, prepare for another type of 100km hike.

11. Carry with you only the bare minimum you will need, keeping in mind unnecessary baggage that will weigh you down.

12. Enjoy the hike. Enjoy the meditative state the hike will bring you.

13. Enjoy the efficiency of your lightness.

14. Such is Life and the 'Backpack of Blame'.

4.
Create
New
Stories

Create new stories until the very last breath, there may exist an opportunity to recount them.

We may believe, as we are repeatedly told, that life is great and full of excitement and opportunities in our twenties or thirties, but not later in life. The stories we start telling about those years in our forties, fifties, and sixties will be stinking stale by the time we are in our seventies, especially if told to the same available and limited audience, usually the people closest to us.

Is anyone actually listening to stale and limited stories? I can say that I do not. Sometimes I may comply as an act of respect, depending on the person telling me the story. Such a story is missing the aura of magic that will make my senses light up and want to embrace my life as a contagious effect caused by the person recounting the story. Is it no wonder that there is not much excitement in really listening to people who are growing older? In using the term 'growing older' here, I am only including people who are caught in their own self-imposed limitations by repeatedly doing what does not serve them or anyone around them. In the absence of their awareness, they miss out on opportunities to seek continuous purpose and possibilities in learning within new territories of the unknown while they accept the belief in being without purpose.

Stories that come from actual events starring your Self in the lead role have a magnetic pull in *Living Older*. It is your responsibility to live stories even if the storyline is nothing unusual. The fact that it stars you and your unique perceptions will attract audiences looking for a particular inspiration. In order to have stories realised from actual events, you will need to live them. In order to have an abundance of stories, you need to continuously create them, and the more you *Live Older*, the richer your chronicle will be.

I do not know how long I will live. No one has access to such information about life expectancy. What I do know is that for every day of life that I get, I have a responsibility to make it the best that I can within my abilities. Many a time, I am required to dig deeper or to adapt to the events around me. The chemistry in being engaged with our vastly changing environment and relationships provides us the energy to live many stories. *Live Older* every day that you get.

Be present facing a new day, not absent in the shadows of looking backwards.

Habits quickly become comfortable. The lack of excitement in new learning possibilities can make us lose our senses, including passion. Instead, we begin to instill within us the fear of the unknown and the ridicule of being a learner at a new task. Soon, our souls, our bodies, and our minds no longer have a chance to experience the newness of anything. Instill the energy of newness and create the next story.

Creating Stories

A Sprinkle of Ideas

1. Start by doing something you would never normally do.

2. Bring back your invisible friends from long ago and find out what happened to them throughout the years

3. Find out what you can do to make someone else's life better.

4. Learn some sentences from a foreign language and travel to the country to use them. See what results you get.

5. Live every moment with all that you have got!

6. Create a business that has an investment of $50 or £50 or €507.

7. Practice *Living Older.*

8. Fear not the ability to feel.

9. Be at the pulse of your community.

10. Identify what is required.

11. Learn the skill. Be the supply to the identified demand.

Believe that there is always someone whose life you will touch.

5.
Wrangle With Courage To Go Where You Have Not Gone Before

A lifetime passes so quickly.

In our twenties, we are excited to finally become adults. We carry with us the illusion that we are finally free to do what we want to do. Oops! We find out soon enough that this is not necessarily true. Before we know it, we get caught up in the 'maybe-will-dos', the 'have-to-dos' and the 'should-dos'. We begin to live for insurance. We start to weave the illusive safety net that will ensure us financially, physically and socially.

There is another path, the one full of weeds because not many use it. To take this path requires courage, a virtue that cannot be bought or secured by the weave of the safety net. The courage to live life lightly and to be at peace with all that is included on the pathways of our life travels. It is the courage to turn away from the herd and to go in the opposite direction if required. It is a scary thing to feel alone and away from the crowds.

Living Older requires you to adopt courage to stand by the value of your life; to correct our wrongs as well as those who we have wronged; to move forward with a thrust and not to remain in the past of what once was; to accept that life is a continuous journey outside of our physical body and mind. Additionally, you need courage to ask for forgiveness and to forgive, to be silly, to make mistakes, to be afraid, to provide strength.

Courage is an ability we all possess, but one we rarely exercise. To invite courage into our stories, we need to move in a direction that is led by our intuition and away from the direction we are taught will keep us comfortable. To allow for the presence of courage, we need to drop daily work that we hate to do, the work we go to every new day with a deeper dread, the job we do not leave because there is nothing else safe and secure to replace it.

Many people choose to live in fear of death. There is such a strong focus on this objective that the present essence of life is put aside. We become easily manipulated into believing the visibly degenerating physical body is equal to the degeneration of the soul as well. We start to believe the value of such a life must be limited in consciousness too. Au contraire! I believe that the soul is enlarging in the physical body as we age. Its presence is bigger than ever. Its purpose on this physical earth is at its most powerful. If only we slow down to feel, to hear, to see within the silence of our own company.

In *Living Older*, we need to challenge the Self to face both our known and unknown fears. We know of its presence but we need to take the time needed to learn the roots of our fears. This is followed by a need to replace the large amounts of fear in our inner software with a high zest for adventure and 'as-yet-to-live' experiences.

When we feel strongly about an idea, a question or a way of being, doubt has a way of creeping in quickly. It comfortably settles alongside all of our untapped brilliance. At such times, an insurgence of a deeper trust is required—a trust in our conscious selves. It is a trust in Self to persevere and to be resourceful although you find yourself in unfamiliar territory based on your consistent history and experience. Trust in the Universe, and what it holds for us after we choose to take the plunge into a new chapter of un-known adventures in living a complete life. There is nothing more powerful than the choice to live well.

It is not the years or the time we have left that drive our lives. It is the way we live our life all the time that provides the rush of adrenaline and the tingling in our senses.

Bring courage up from deep inside of you and do all the good things you need to do. Get on a natural high with life now, do not stop . . . ever!

Seek More Courage

Start Here

Acquire skills that you can exchange for cash or barter for room and board as you travel from place to place.

Check in with your Self to ensure that you are content. Contentment does not mean that you have all the material things you are told you need. This is a feeling you have deep within you.

If you have feelings of discontentment, spend time with them. They have come to you as lessons or as opportunities for you to expand your consciousness further.

Affirm the choice for a path that serves your life and in so doing, the path that has not served your life will be destroyed and replaced. It is not you who will be destroyed in making this move.

There are two different choices in making a decision: the comfortable and easy one or the uncomfortable and difficult one.

The only limitations available to you are the ones you have placed for your Self.

Have courage to be silly.

Have courage to not know it all.

Make new mistakes in new territories not old mistakes in old territories.

6.
Be The Boss Of Your Inspiration

Inspiration is a smooth sounding word.

Whatever its classical or structured definition, it needs a private interpretation for each individual person who is touched by its magnetic effect. It is an awesome word and experience available to every human soul. Higher education, money, age, status or job title has no influence on its availability.

Inspiration provides a confirmation, an acknowledgement that the choices we have made in living a life may have a positive impact on the lives of others. Inspiration requires no force and it cannot be forced. It has to happen naturally without superficial effort, similar to a polarity that will either attract or repel.

Knowledge of inspiration can be a result of noise, talk and discussion. Action of inspiration, on the other hand, happens with subtleness and in quietude.

Inspiration cannot be practiced or acquired. It is a translation of deeds and ways of being that are understood by those who needed the understanding. Inspiration does not concern uniformity. It is individual and unique by design. It also comes with a sensual warm feeling that feels like every cell in the body is being soaked in the first warm rays of sunshine after a cold, frosty winter.

In *Living Older*, it is time to consider a possibility that we may have lived our life seeking inspiration, not knowing that it was in our Self all along. In living life with the quest to acquire all the knowledge and all the material wealth in the world, we may have unknowingly attracted envy instead of inspiration. Being envious of someone is not inspiration. *Living Older* requires that we seek to spread inspiration like a contagious sense of ease, a rhythm that moves to the sound of "Inspire...be inspired..., inspire...be inspired...".

When inspiration lies dormant and numb due to loud distracting noises surrounding our daily thoughts, we choose to look for endless entertainment and stories on our electronic devices instead of moving and operating with our innate ability to create something with our minds, our hands and our spirit, and in being of good use to Self and to others.

In *Living Older* it is never too late to explore what it is that life provides uniquely to us, and to affirm our own personal inspirations as a reaction to our experiences in living. It is the perfect time to be 'touched' by another being's life choices, and to acquire the extra super charged fuel that confirms a language understood between souls.

Be inspiration. Wash off the judgements, both your own and those you adopt from others. When in the presence of inspiration, you will begin to value its presence and its ability to affect others. By itself, inspiration has no value. It is not a word or an act that can be bought. It is an experience that can only be felt at the level of the soul.

Wear the glow of inspiration with a balance of both pride and humility. Be the catalyst of inspiration for another. Soak in the glory of inspiration. Do more of what inspires you. Own it as an opportunity to feed your soul.

Years that pass filled with inspiration are priceless in comparison to a life that passes in years of accumulating emptiness.

Finding Inspiration

Start Here

Ways To Inspire

Questions to Consider

1. Seek inspiration within Self. Learn the ability to look inward before looking outward.

2. Take the time you need. Slow down. There is no strategy available for universal magic to happen.

3. Celebrate the inspiration you discover. Know that it is uniquely yours.

4. There is no comparability scale for inspirations. Each passing moment, constantly shifting environments and every new breath will change its intention and presence. Similarities are similarities. Similarities are not identical.

5. Pass it on to another or others. The value of inspiration is in what it means to another person. The identity and the language of how you inspire another may have nothing to do with the inspiration you need from someone else.

6. Your inspiring light is not meant to attract everyone. It is not a tool for attention seeking.

1. What is considered inspiration for the youth of today?

2. What is considered inspiration for the elders of today?

3. What is the value of your presence in the world today?

4. Do you know your inspiring qualities?

5. Have you taken ownership of these qualities?

6. How does your life inspire change?

Start small, be authentic and prepare for the surprise!

When you perform a thought or an act in the presence of your soul, and you commit to doing it wholeheartedly without seeking praise or reward while remaining authentic to your Self, you invite inspiration.

Become An Entrepreneur

The word *entreprendre* in French means to undertake something. There is a distinctive difference between 'to do' and 'to undertake'. 'Undertaking' connotes having taken on something with a relevant amount of consideration.

As an entrepreneur, one undertakes an idea to create a demand or an opportunity to supply a demand, both conscious and unconscious, from the potential customer. It is accompanied by a strong need, a passion, a belief that fuels this undertaking. It includes the importance in doing it under the responsibility of Self so as to create an exchange for cash or something of monetary value. Hopefully, other individuals, one or many with varying expertise, will work together with this entrepreneur to share common objectives.

Entrepreneurship is related to business, but it is rarely related to inspiration. In *Living Older*, be curious about entrepreneurship. Make a difference in many other people's lives, including your own, by creating a business idea that fills a need where it is required. Learn all you need to know. If you already have the experience in entrepreneurship, undertake it differently this time. Use the available freedom to stretch your limits. Invite fear to be an acquaintance that does not worry you. Use entrepreneurship to create a community of people who work together making goodness for people, while living the work they do with you as they would live life outside of it.

Be an inspiration for yourself. Be an inspiration for the energy that is contained within you. Enjoy what you do and never call it work.

Ready, Set, Go!

7.
Wear
A New Pair
Of Eyes
Every Day

Every day we are bombarded with information.

On the tube in London or the MRT in Singapore, people choose to drown themselves with information from ill news to Vines to photos to the behaviour of cats and dogs. We are fed information that wounds the soul or that overexcites us. We allow no time to mourn loss, death, pain or suffering. Instead, we quickly replace this valuable opportunity for depth and for increasing humanity with violent games for entertainment, and as food for our starving consciousness.

It is almost as if we are afraid to be alone with our own consciousness.

The design of our environment initiates judgment and criticism from within us about information for which we actually and truly do not have the experience or enough knowledge about for appropriate reactions. Yet, we react constantly as if automatically triggered. Mostly, we react inefficiently in the absence of consciousness. Because we are blessed with the rapid acquisition of almost any information, we grab at it unaware of the accompanying emotional roller coaster ride. Simultaneously, we are cursed with the inability of our excluded consciousness to process the quality and the depth of the tsunami of information coming our way. In a similar manner, we gobble our food to satisfy our over-sensitised mouths with no consideration for the rest of the larger and more important systems within our body that will provide or fail to provide us with what we need to live well.

As we add up the numbers in our years of life, all the stray information, judgements, unofficially adopted ideas and other such things, have multiplied in our beings. We become a living library that is keen on sourcing useless and emotion-squeezing information.

It is not easy to physically and mentally limit the 'loud noise' of information that enters our personal space. In *Living Older*, we need to apply intention to add a conscious screen, as we may do to prevent mosquitoes from entering a tropical home. Intention is needed to create a vital opportunity for assimilation of information before we send it further into our body as digested material that becomes a part of who we are and what we believe.

A conscious awareness is recommended to create filtration systems. As we *Live Older*, there is a need to see the actions and the reactions of the world we live in from the capacity of our very own eyes and from what they process as judgements with the rest of our beings. If the vision is blurry, it is time to adjust the lens by never stopping to learn. If the vision is a perfect 20/20, it is time to source a groovy pair of sunglasses.

Work is required to slow down the delivery of our own judgements in areas where we have insufficient or zero expertise. We must develop strength in ourselves to prevent us from adopting the high frequency and contagious perceptions, as well as the judgements, of others.

I am a visual learner and simultaneously, a contact lens user. There is profound benefit in the idea of changing my eyes for a fresh new pair every day. It allows for an automatic reset of visuals as to how I reacted or how I saw an event just the day before. The ritual reminds me that I make mistakes. It reminds me that I have a RESET button in order to start again. Each new start creates an opportunity for me to be better. The ritual extends the ability to visually install a screen that allows for a conscious reflection on any event and its accompanying global or individual judgements, before allowing it to become a part of my holistic being.

Every new day is a clean slate for a new thought or a new way of looking at an old thought.

If our eyes are truly the windows to our soul, then what it sees today needs to be selective. We need to exchange the controls to self-command for what it needs to see versus what is being enticed upon us to see. In the life of a day, we witness so many scenes visually. Accordingly, we feel and absorb nuances of varied emotions.

We make assumptions, for example, about people we meet, assumptions that are a result of what we may have read or of what we have been told by others. In the conflict of emotions, we doubt ourselves. Based on what we see and what we are made to believe, we may overestimate or underestimate ourselves as well as others. We experience an array of emotions that affect our energy. We worry about new problems and old problems that have now become habits. By the end of the day, our invisible baggage is a heavy load for our souls to bear.

Using a visual of 'removing your old eyes' before you sleep and 'putting on new ones' when you wake up will allow you to remember that a new day is a new start. Use this little ritual to reset both your physical and conscious vision through infiltration. It will provide you with the ability to discard what does not serve you, thereby creating the possibility to increase energy for selective and purposeful information.

Living Older is about living new ways of being that serve us in exchange for old ways of being that we know do not serve us.

Be careful in exchanging a pair of new eyes daily! Do not make the mistake of removing your sight entirely. When you possess 'in-sight-ful' eyes, you are accorded the ability to see the difference between the truth and the lies, the ability to see the oppressed, to see your brainwaves being side-tracked.

Live Older and never hide comfortably behind an excuse to be voluntarily blind.

In order to seal the ritual of purposefully wearing new eyes, commit to stop talking about what you do not like in the world in which you live.

Instead, commit to creating the world we need to live in by being a conscious light.

How to Remove a Pair of Eyes and How to Put On a New Pair of Eyes Daily

1. Select a comfortable place. **2.** A quiet place will be helpful. **3.** Sit up with your shoulders relaxed and downward.

11. Continue to inhale and to exhale with intention and in silence. **10.** Visualise your Self voluntarily removing the imaginary mask off your eyes, together with all the information you do not need for your Self. **9.** Store this valuable information in your immediate memory.

12. Express gratitude. **13.** Sleep light. Sleep well. **14.** Upon waking up, and while still in bed, be conscious of your breath as you inhale and exhale and be in gratitude for your night's sleep and the ability to rest and to re-energise.

4. Inhale and exhale with intention.

5. Visualise an eye mask and place it over your eyes.

6. In the silence, your mind may start to replay some thoughts, voices, concepts, noise and other such features that we will call information. In the case your mind does not replay these features, proceed to turn them on for yourself by replaying some influential parts of your day.

8. Consciously select the information retrieved during the process that will serve you in *Living Older.*

7. At some point, you will feel satisfied with all that your eyes, ears and senses processed for the day.

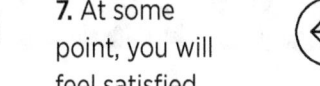

15. Use imagery to visualise your Self, putting on a new pair of eyes. If you wear contact lenses, the ritual is enhanced with your added consciousness.

16. Make a silent commitment to absorb and to stream only what will serve you.

17. Practice this ritual as a reminder that you are choosing to see things differently.

8.
Celebrate Your Nakedness

Being Naked.

There is a great deal of controversy about skin and parts of the body. How they are incorporated in life is largely dependent on culture, upbringing and personal choices that we need to comprehend on a deeper level. The physical body, with clothes or without clothes, is truly the abode of the soul. We come into this world in it and live in it as our lifelong vessel, and we die in its occupation. Our physical body is the only one we have throughout our lifetime.

Being naked is the art of removing all the decorative and camouflaging layers of expectations, both of Self and of others. Being naked is a reminder of how you came into this world, and of how we truly will leave it. It is the raw connection with all natural sensations, a playful reminder that we are sensually alive. Being naked with the environment —the sensual feeling of fresh water on your bare skin.

There is a surviving need for two distinctive types of bodies: the male body and the female body. Each body is creatively designed as unique and amazing art forms. The primal purpose of the different bodies remains a constant same: to reproduce.

The way we look at the naked physical body is an enigma in itself. Each culture, each community, each family, each individual has a personal way of looking at it from an entirely different perspective.

By choosing to *Live Older*, it is time to accept our nakedness. It is time to lay down our weapons against being bodily accepted within a very limited template. It is time to invest in its loving care. As the time of our lives has accrued, our bodies have experienced countless stories, adventures and transformations that tell of a physical vessel that has carried the soul. My body has represented me for all that I present to the exterior world of my Self.

Being naked invites Self as the audience.

If you have never liked your body, time is long overdue to make peace with it and to look at your naked body. The space is your sacred space, and it is time to be naked with your Self, physically, emotionally, and spiritually. It is a time to be truly grateful for the physical body that has accompanied you through the passing of time. There is no room here for the judgement, opinion or advice of another person, no matter how close they are to you.

When you are able to look at yourself naked in the mirror, you will feel a primal power supporting you in your physical presence and a sense of ownership will begin to develop. In being naked, there are no disguises in the form of clothes, accessories or makeup and there is no differentiating between expensive or cheap. Only you are present, naked as you first came into this world.

Get in touch with your wrinkles, lines and excesses and allow them to tell their stories. Touch your scars and let them remind you of what your body endured through life's adventures. Acknowledge your greying hair as the wisdom in the changing seasons.

External comments regarding your body and your nakedness are allowed by invitation only. If there is judgement and criticism, you need to settle your condition by choosing not to carry the weight of another's words. If there is judgement from within, it is time to clear the air with your naked Self. Being naked with yourself is an important time to be grateful for the body that has served you, and that continues to serve you, as the residence of your soul and for your consciousness.

It is time to touch our bodies with kindness, for all of the different ways we may have tried to hide it with shame, and for how we may have abused it.

The body is a strong visual reminder of what we truly own. Being naked with our bodies is the time for truth in the acceptance of Self.

9.
Allow The Freedom To Laugh At Your Self

No matter the age, at some point in our lives, we may have been afflicted with the curse of the misunderstanding that being laughed at was akin to a big bad thing; an unwanted and unattractive stigma to carry around, an event that was attached to some form of disgrace or of being ridiculed. These are possible reasons that make us get up quickly from a fall in a public area while pretending that nothing actually happened. Perhaps it is why we fight really hard to keep ourselves from laughing at someone else who we witness falling in a public area (the little falls and trips not the serious ones). We have to try so hard to contain the escaping laughter our body naturally needs to let out!

The most beautiful thing I find about not living up to someone else's expectations is the ability to truly laugh at myself when I do something silly or something apparently embarrassing.

The reason for this is the power of my presence remains mine and it is not lost to someone else and their opinions. If the event actually embarrassed me, laughing at it allows the awkward feeling to pass quickly without hurting myself emotionally.

Have you ever wondered, dear reader, why laughing at yourself is considered so bad? If the natural symphony of our subconscious needs to break out in laughter, why do we try to control it at a superficial level? The answer may be that we are all expected to be perfect beings, who can never make mistakes, or who can never be in a situation that looks anything short of perfect. It is no wonder that so many of us act like we are painted in multiple coats of varnish that prevent us from a simple or a heartfelt loud laugh, depending only on intoxicating substances as a justifiable excuse to let loose trapped emotions that will allow us to feel that we are human.

To *Live Older*, we must laugh. The best laughs are the ones we aim freely at ourselves, not in mockery of someone else, but laughing in celebration of our imperfect abilities. The only way we can truly laugh at Self in order to heal our soul is by venturing outside of our comfort areas and into unknown territories requiring us to be new and naïve, to learn in new ways, to meet new people in places where we do not reign in familiarity.

Seek the opportunity to start off a nervous laughter. Create many perfect moments to find an endless amount of reasons to laugh an uncontrollable heartfelt laugh. With a free spirit and a daily practice, you will be laughing loudly at yourself in little time. In so doing, you are reminded of being alive. You will be set free momentarily from the worldly grip of false perfections in order to be in celebration with your imperfections.

Start by laughing at some imperfect experiences of Self, follow it by finding someone who will allow you to share similar experiences.

Create a ridiculous party!

10.
Own Your Health And Its Wellness. Know How To Operate Its Care

We live in a time when individual health and wellbeing seems to be everyone else's property, except our very own.

Our wellbeing is a commodity that can be traded to the highest bidder in terms of its care.

We are blessed to be in a time when skilled doctors and caregivers are available in life-threatening situations, such as accidents and some major health conditions. We owe them our gratitude for the years and years of learning and their dedicated years of experience in trauma and rehabilitation. In the context of this book; however, we are referring to health at a level of personal care, the type required before any illness sets up house in our living organism.

Our body is a fascinating entity. There are so many different orchestrations playing in perfect harmony at any one time.

This perfection functions between optimal balance and an acute imbalance. The life we live, today, has many effects on our health causing both positive and negative implications. Visualise the work of an air traffic controller who is synchronising the many different flights that are flying at any one given time. Their expertise has to be accurate regarding flights in their air space. If they are not paying attention to each detail or if they are not listening to communications from the many individual flights flying over their air space there is an increased possibility for accidents. Our bodies, too, have an amazing system of communication.

It will begin to cause reactions, consequences and symptoms that appear naturally when we do something to cause it pain, or when we ingest food and drink that it interprets as poisonous to our individual chemistry. Often, we are not listening to the beginnings of these events, keeping us from connecting a history of cause and effect pertaining to our own bodies.

Among the daily practices I hold dear, the one pertaining to self-care in body, mind and soul wins miles ahead of all else. Feeding myself right is the only powerful choice I have to give my life the best chance it needs.

In being disconnected from our bodies, we have come to believe only an educated and qualified mind has the capacity regarding the wellness of Self. There is an urgent need to come back to our core where resides an innate awareness concerning individual feeling and interpretations in the state of personal wellness. There is an urgent need to bring back respect for the inner voices of our body's communicating channels, long before we are seriously ill.

We need to awaken Awareness, Innate Wisdom and Consciousness from deep within us.

These are skills and wisdom that belong to an inner expertise that is designed to accompany the operational manual of our body. When I eat something and my stomach bloats, a communication system warns me that my body is reacting to what I just consumed. If I choose to ignore it by continuing to consume this food that is causing an unpleasant reaction, the discomfort starts to morph into another symptom, which will proceed towards a more serious imbalance for my body.

In *Living Older*, we acknowledge our bodies are changing as they have been designed to do. A changing body does not always equal a weaker body unless the unique and individual care for it is completely ignored. These changes are intricate and individual; however, the common denominator remains change. Each one of us is different, and the difference is equipped with a tailor-made awareness that fits our uniqueness.

In order to *Live Older*, I need to consider that my current state of body, emotion and mind is a culmination of all the past years of care or abuse. It is not bestowed upon me suddenly just because I am increasing in chronological years. Of course, every individual being has an intricately varied story different from mine, which explains why diets work differently and only for a limited time for everyone.

In order to design the years in *Living Older* better, I need to invest time to determine what has not worked for me in terms of my maximum health potential. I need to connect with my inner body wisdom so as to be very sensitive to its communication with me concerning all that I feed it: all of my senses and emotions, the environment I live in, as well as the origins of food and drink I consume in the name of sustenance or entertainment.

Learn and practice how to retrieve the inner knowledge of your health awareness.

Be accurate in listening to its communication methods via mild to acute symptoms. Add voice to its communication when handing your health over to another caregiver. Learn to associate the difference between what makes the body and mind feel stronger and what makes it weaker. Take ownership of your individual wellness. It is the most important investment we make. My commitment to *Living Older* precedes any other life-enriching idea I have.

If what I eat is truly who I am, I need to feed my body with life not with death.

11.
Explore The Power That Comes With Age

Power is not only about weapons and physical strength.

On the other side of our beliefs concerning power is the example of a little shoot pushing itself out of a seed, or the ability in birthing a human being. The natural state of becoming older has been tranquillised to a passive, dependent and deteriorating process. We have allowed the super powers of 'older' to be removed and for its purpose to be buried in the oblivion of ignorance. We have then enveloped it with a great deal of negative passive energy by considering it to be 'boring', 'stationary', and 'stagnant'. Passive energy can be very positive and powerful as well. Meditation, quietness, aware-ness and the understanding of consciousness are all passive in nature, but they quietly contain the active bubbles of positive action, like the state of water just before it boils.

We inherit a world in which we further create and procreate. From the moment of birth, there is an invisible path designed by us humans, a path full of expectations laid out before us. This path merges with the paths of other beings as we begin the process of a silent, competitive race of consumption and financial accumulation. If we choose to have a family, the pathway extends towards more expectations, more consuming possibilities, more financial accumulation, and very soon, some form of debt.

The general design of our societies, today, focuses mostly around maximising these pathways for us until we are older. If we are no longer working to accumulate more cash, chances are high that we are contained in a limited space in the name of 'care' or that we are 'let out to pasture' until we die.

There are no cool trains leaving for the town called Older!

In keeping within the intention of this book, let us not look at 'the wrongs' and 'the rights' of how we currently operate as a society. Instead, let us focus our attention on the formulation of a grand individual —The Self.

Whatever our individual choices are in providing, surviving, bringing up a family or the accumulation of material things, at some point, we will arrive at a place of redundancy. You may no longer be required at a job you did seemingly forever as a full-time parent, caregiver or employee. It seems that we arrive, all too suddenly, at a place of limited expectations for valuable exchanges while we are still very much alive. Depending on who we are, the allure of eternal holidays seems like a wondrous reward in arriving at this phase in life. But how long can one happily have a limited purpose?

In *Living Older*, a time of immense power, we have to learn to create a new phase of growth. In the resumé of living an entire life, the experience in having lived many life years needs to be considered as highly valuable. An innate value comes to us with the experience of actually squeezing life for all of its vital juices; not the superficial experience we get from acquiring a white coat to put on as a self-proclaimed status symbol. The value of this experience increases with every weakness that is strengthened, and every idea of purpose that is created in freedom from hierarchy, for the entire world to benefit.

The world needs creative ideas to assist in its healing. The value of such experience becomes priceless when we start to number the multiple mistakes made in exploring life. There is power in this experience. It is the power of the higher consciousness. It is the power to create anything without a spotlight of expectations.

Living Older is not a time to quietly fade into the sunset. It is a time to be aware of the power available in the quiet strength and abundant creative energy available for solutions to the negative outcomes that everyone else in the rat race is too blind to see, or possibly has no time to be enlightened.

In choosing to *Live Older*, we must reclaim a lost power of the elders, a once upon a time honour in many ancient cultures. The power to connect with a higher consciousness, the power to heal from stress, the power to apply patience and determination and the confidence to remain grounded. We need to consciously choose where to invest this powerful energy. It is not a time for arrogant lectures on how others should live their lives. A life journey for every individual is a private and individual choice. This type of unwanted advice depletes our conscious energy and it has no positive purpose.

It is a time to inspire, a time to use the strengths of your life experiences including the references of both your good and bad choices, to inspire in deed rather than in words only. Use this experience to build, to create, to vitalise areas of your humanity that have remained stagnant and are beginning to rot in their uselessness. The energy available in *Living Older* is a moving energy. It is not a passive or stagnant energy.

Our matured energy needs to go toward making things happen. It is not a passive energy of 'wait and see'. It is a time to discover the power of a new energy that is only available with the presence of both intent and action. It is a time to have the courage to venture, collectively or individually, into areas of thought and creation that have been abandoned, not because of a lack of importance, but due to the lack of attractiveness in financial accumulation, an overabundance of glorified expectations and in the lack of their consumer value.

In order to enhance this innate power, it is important to start your venture by being deeply silent. It is important to access a deep wisdom that resides in all of us. In order to go there, you need to retrain your Self. Learn new ways to learn. Adopt a different way of being that provides great purposeful energy and contentment in simplicity that values material needs less and conscious needs more.

Do not misunderstand this power. It is not a power to be used in proving yourself as better than another. It is not a power for the ego to be right by pushing this righteousness onto others.

It is a rooted power that stays firm in the familiar dance of chaos and constant 'change' that has become mightier in the many years of Living Older.

It is time to create adaptability in an environment of constant uncertainty. When you are good friends with adaptability, you will love its company in times of transformation and unexpected outcomes. The ability to adapt is a vital tool when you are caught in a fierce storm in the ocean of life. It is a super tool that allows you to survive the many varying and unpredictable moods of life's storms. Adaptability provides you with abilities to move according to the rhythm of music that life is playing at anytime.

A Side Story

When I was much younger, one of my older sisters would ask me to run errands for her. This involved mostly doing what she wanted me to do whether I liked it or not. If I refused, she would answer, 'I am older than you. You have to do this for me!' I always found her answer extremely unfair even as a much younger child. Increased chronological age does not equal respect because of a larger number.

Living Older requires that you become a practicing example in living a life. Wear the coat of honour in every aspect of your living life. Become respect as much as you require respect.

You are wisdom only if you continue to learn, not because of what you once knew.

12. Food. What Goes In Me Becomes Me

There are so many possibilities when choosing a life of Living Older: New ideas to adopt, older ideas to retranslate, exciting projects to create, and an ability to design a continuous and complete life of purpose that will be lived. However, while it is true that you have the possibility of choice, a larger truth remains that the physical body and the mind, by Nature's design, are growing older and changing as part of the circle of life.

It is an honour to accept this truth rather than battling it because any other idea will continue to keep us in a haze of useless illusions that do not serve us to live the adventures of life optimally. The limited life span of this cycle provides each one of us with the reminder that life is truly beautiful and unknowingly short. It is up to each of us human beings to do what we deem to be important in the ownership of life while we still have it. As soon as you accept this truth, use some newly learned skills and the power of being alive to make strategic changes for dynamic efficiency in the operations of your physical body and mind, and to be in tune with Nature's law.

If we are what we eat, we need to learn new lessons on the importance of what and how we feed ourselves. Food is not eaten only to satiate the senses of the tongue, although under the spell of a holistic imbalance, the unconscious Self leaves the body and mind, asking for nothing more while it starves from malnourishment.

Food directly provided to you from Nature is the perfect gift for you to benefit in your life adventures, while keeping you introspective and connected to its rich and gloriously complicated soil, oceans and skies that share the bloodline through chlorophyll and other minute and miraculous chemistry.

Alternatively, food can also be a man-made concoction for personal profit that we feed ourselves in return for some cheap thrills from our limited and highly spoilt senses in the service of our likes and our likes alone. Food is not food only consumed as meals. Food is the information I absorb and store in my brain, and food is also the music I listen to that nourishes the depths of my soul. When I sing a song whose lyrics are demeaning to humankind, I am feeding on its negative energy. The people I choose to surround myself with for the quantity and the quality of love, care and friendship are my nourishment as food. Food becomes me, however and whatever it is I choose to be.

In *Living Older*, we will relearn lessons about what our mind and body need in terms of food for life versus food for death. We need to listen with new ears. We need to see with new eyes. We need to be in connection with quality food sources. Food is what we need to fuel our dreams. Food is what we need to keep our physical selves able, and our souls dancing.

When we choose to understand, respect and honour the value of what Nature provides us, the planet will require no more saving.

In keeping at optimal levels of your individual self, you have the ability to *Live Older*. In the thirteen years of work as a holistic nutritionist, I have only just begun to truly experience how food transforms into becoming me. I have seen my Self transform from ineffective to effective in weeks of changing my eating habits. Likewise, I have needed the experience of going from being effective to an ineffective performance of Self as a result of the food I consumed. The way I feed myself and what I eat are my most important self-imposed standards that I need to meet in order to really fully live life's adventures as my body changes through its required seasons.

Food for Thought in Living Older

Based on personal and professional experiences

Throughout this book, the word *food* represents both food and drink.

All food is not equal.

Chemistry in individuals is not created the same.

Feeding the digestive system may result in better wellness than feeding the taste buds in the mouth alone.

Seeking to feed on quality foods provided by Nature is the most important investment you make for yourselves and for the planet that we will pass on to the next generations of conscious living beings.

The body and mind change constantly. The way you eat varies according to your surrounding environment, your mood and your culture, as well as the change in seasons, your personal transitions and even the phase of the moon may be affecting what you choose to eat!

Any food that takes away energy from you can be immediately exchanged for foods that bring energy to you.

Food can turn you on or turn you off.

Highly addictive foods and tumultuous emotions love to tango as partners.

There is no one perfect way to eat.

The choice in the foods we eat affects everyone else on the planet.

Food is pleasure. This sensual experience is not defined by taste buds alone.

The current state of your physical and mental body is not a sudden curse of old age. It is a natural result in years of investment put towards its care, similar, to a savings account in a bank. If you save good cash regularly, even a small amount would increase in number as the years of savings are added. If you did not put any cash into your savings account, there is no investment aside from wishful thinking.

Food has the ability to convert into a superpower.

What You Eat Becomes You

A Sprinkle of Alternative, Out-of-Food Experiences

1. Listen to a recording of someone talking or recounting a story for at least four hours everyday for at least five days. This is done without voluntary resistance to the outcome of the exercise. Notice how you speak by the sixth day. You will notice that you have adopted some of the speaker's expressions, accents or mannerisms.

2. Immerse your Self in a culture that is different from yours for a few months. It is better if you do not speak the same language. You will notice that you have picked up mannerisms of the culture without any conscious effort.

3. Seek out negative stories to read everyday (not very difficult to do today) for a few weeks. Notice how easy it will be for you to adopt a negative stance. The exercise applies beautifully to positive stories, too.

4. Love yourself everyday and notice how you become more proactive in owning your Self.

A Side Story

As a holistic nutritionist, I experience how I become the energy of the food I consume. I am referring to the energy or a personality I believe is innate in every living being with the capacity to be translated into the 'living' life of the person consuming it with a conscious presence.

When I set out for a walk after eating potato or corn crisps, my lungs and my body begin to feel like I am wearing bags of cement, a very heavy feeling that slows me down. If I set out to walk after eating greens and other real foods, my body feels like it is on rocket fuel with a reserve that seems stocked up with endless energy.

13.
Create or Discover New Thoughts On Ways Of Being

We can change for the better or for the worse.

Anticipating a change for the better creates a joyous feeling of hope as if better things really are to come. In creating an effort to make this happen, talking change is a lot easier than 'being the change'. Our human nature loves the illusion of words and what they represent. Unavoidably, such words are hollow without the partnering of experienced actions. The emptiness in these words rolls out of mouths without the authenticity of the soul.

In order to create a new way of *Living Older*, and in order to walk in its less travelled path, change has to take place. This is a change that is not desired by all of humankind who will continue to grow older. In not welcoming this natural change of our life's seasons, which will occur, we deplete our energy by fighting a force that is much more powerful than we will ever be.

Life is not meant to suit all of our individual wants, even though it seems like it sometimes. For some of us, this is unacceptable. I once asked the Universe, 'what is it I am meant to do? If there is something I am here to do, please let me know'. A few months later, I was pregnant with my second child after thirteen years. Four months after she was born, the doctor told me I had about a month to live following the diagnosis of an actively spreading cancer. Life, as I knew it and as I wanted to know it, was no longer the same. My decision without knowing the outcome was to take charge of my Self and to live, no matter the time limit. I survived. I did not just survive, which is an immense gift in itself; I survived with a heightened sensibility for how to live my life.

Accepting change and its many transformations are non-compromising and compulsory requirements for those of us who want to *Live Older* purposely and consciously.

In order for deep transformations to take place, you need to lose your control over it. You need to be present in silence as it teaches you what you have not learnt before.

The cells in your body and mind dance in excitement from the thrill of having your current limits pushed into new levels of experiences and sensual pleasures. The alternative is to continue in the monotonous current residing in the repetitive habits that provide little fuel for the soul. Any path of change is full of unknown challenges. It is occupied by a high probability of difficulties and roadblocks as you venture into areas where no GPS exists. This is a good enough reason for many to not take the way of change.

The negativity in growing older surrounds us due to an abundance of information and experience in living as 'anti' age. This is not the choice for my wild soul. I need to design my life to include continuous contributions and purposeful actions without the exaggerations of negativity weighing down my possibilities surrounding the time of being older. In choosing to *Live Older*, this requirement is a compulsory one. It must replace the current design built on a predetermined end of a human life as sickly and without purpose.

These new thoughts and ways of being may seem radical because they are ideas that expand on living rather than ideas that surround dying, and any idea of change is not accepted by everyone. The decision to accept this change in mind-set is clearly outside of being simply a logical or an illogical one. A decision such as this has to be led by a deep feeling within us that is committed to the connection of life that is bigger than our worldly possessions.

Ideas for change in *Living Older* may require a great deal of trial and error. The quest is not in the search for a perfect size that fits all sizes of individual souls. In my case, it is my wild soul saying, 'Let us not stop playing'! I make a commitment to my soul to create an exciting playground where I can venture toward constant uncertainty, explore new places and people, feel the roller coaster of the emotions of living, make mistakes I have never made before, and pick myself up to try again and again and again.

Get a little lost. Feel comfortable in not knowing everything. Use your instincts. Retrain your mind to discover new ways of being and doing.

Life Versions 1 & 2

Life Version 1

You are born, bred, and educated to make money.

The commencement of the START line varies depending on culture or family. You start running the race of 'Money as Life' immediately; after all, the faster you can make more money, the better your life.

You start out believing you are making money for yourself and your loved ones and you convince yourself you need the money to satisfy the constantly enlarging 'needs' you are being told you need—Every second. Every day.

Your resumé is a great reflection of life in this version. There are no resumés required to question how many good deeds you have accomplished and how you intend to give back to the planet you are visiting. Such questions are unimaginable in a life that is hyped around the idea of 'who makes more cash gets more'! Really? Get more of what?

At some point, you may arrive at a time when you are no longer able to make this money for yourself. You may become disabled, or you became old, and you are shattered because your self-worth was tagged to that money-making work.

'Oh my! We are sorry, but you need to step aside from this race now. There are too many people in it for us to consider you and your expired ability to be qualified for this race', said the big chief of the 'Money of Life' race, as you and your life begin to crumble around you.

Life Version 2

You are born unique. This ends the need for competition immediately.

How can two unique people compete with each other? Ideally, they will complement each other, a useful ability for creating a larger whole. You are engrained with a living truth that death can happen at any time. In this knowledge, you are aware the longer you get to live, the more purposeful your life at any age. You received a free ticket to be in this life and you know that you will leave it with nothing material that you earned, collected or created on this planet. You realise you have choices, both good and bad. You always have a choice and this complicates life sometimes because it requires that you take action rather than wait in a comfort zone, feeling safe. In this version of a life, the choices available assist in keeping you on the right path like the North on a compass.

Money is necessary as a tool for exchange for only what is necessary while we barter on this man-made system. You are smart. You are creative. You can earn money while being in the constant company of your soul and its life purpose here on the planet as the priceless experience. You are not on the relentless quest for cash to acquire a bottomless pit of unneeded needs. Being older signifies that you were gifted more time to do what you need to do, and the responsibility not to be dis-eased as an after-effect from the race of relentless materialism.

When there is no race, there is time to smell the roses. There is time to understand the hidden values of weeds. There is time to notice that the planet and its inhabitants who are not able to generate an economy are being murdered and abused. In this life version, it is possible to stop these things from happening.

How To Seek Abundant Change

A Sprinkle of Little Ideas

1. Provide useful work for yourself until the end of this physical journey.

2. Learn the many things you do not know.

3. Listen.

4. Love being in silence.

5. Create a whole new range of possible work options outside of the rat race sectors.

6. Be in union with youth and young adults in their early twenties. Share our commonalities in creating a different world or a different way of living on our planet.

7. Represent animals and plants and trees that have no governments and; therefore, no voice for their cause.

8. Create masterpieces in fashion that is particular to the requirements of this specific age.

9. Inspire health in each other using novel and creative manners.

10. Enlarge the community of many individual selves to being a community of love and support, care and companionship.

11. Know that you create your own limitations.

14.
Resexatate™
Your Self

Sex is a simple word.

It is an act available to any being with life running through their veins. It is a word that can simultaneously have an extremely negative connotation as much as an extremely positive one. In the context of this book, I am referring to sex as a healthy, enjoyable experience between two consenting people. Sex is also known as making love, where an ultimate art form is created in the presence of respect, care and sensual touch. The art of making love is an art practiced in the private domains of the people involved. Imagination, fantasy, play, and other such accompaniments provide a palette full of ideas to make this experience unique, and one of utmost fun and satisfaction.

Sex, as a daily word and an action in today's speak is used mostly to represent body bits and pieces, often carrying with it the idea of "seize and take" for extreme temporary pleasure. Whatever one's personal issues may be in regards to sex and other people's opinions about it, we are narrowing the spotlight on sex that is sensual and extremely enjoyable. As such, the result brings with it an energetic glow and an overwhelming feeling of love, respect and an incomparable connection between the people involved.

A sexual being is generally visualised as someone who is young, virile, and good looking. This makes good sense since sex is the ultimate act of attraction designed by Nature for procreation. It is equally important in marketing goods for the sole purpose of monetary profit. This visual is a guaranteed success when the objective is to sell illusions of inadequacy to people whose consciousness is asleep, and to get them to believe that they are forever underachieving.

Sex is a primal function. On the other hand, sexual pleasure is an art form designed by individuals. Individual art cannot be loved by all or hated by none.

There is no one size that fits all.

As the number of years increase, you are made to believe that your physical functions are limited. For example, an older man may develop difficulties to become hard or to ejaculate and an older woman may lose all interest. Depending on how we look at our life transformations, we can either believe that all that was once good and fun has officially ended or we can seize the opportunity to stretch our imagination in rediscovering new territories within our transformations for sensual pleasure. These can be a discovery for some of us as much as for others possibilities to stretch the imagination farther. We are all unique as humans, there is no one text book that can cover all of our individual attributes.

Concerning sexual pleasures, not physical limitations, sheer boredom and a lack of creativity are possible candidates for a sexual shutdown. There is no one source of pleasure, a vital ingredient, in the recipe of a successful sexual partnership. Discovery, curiosity, and imagination are not easily available to those who want them as quickies; therefore, as one grows older, it is so much easier to blame the unhealthy, lacklustre state of our beings as a side effect of being older.

In *Living Older*, we create new experiences in sexual pleasures. It is the perfect time to shift the focus on sex from expectations and lifelong habits to creative play and pleasure. We begin by making sex slow and sensual. We continue by shifting orgasm from physical parts into sensual realms. Because the need to procreate is done and rested, actual intercourse is no longer the ultimate goal and limitation. Foreplay and sensual touch will become the large and new field of sensual and creative play.

Creativity becomes a key requirement in exploring the senses and in evoking touch. In celebration of this new game of pleasure, I present a new and created word for a resuscitated idea that comes with it: **Resexatate**™ - to bring back into existence, or to create new ideas for the art of sex that is no longer attached to the primal requirement of procreation. The conditions of which must include imagination, playfulness, touch, emotion, respect and a celebration of the sense of being alive.

Up until now, sex as a word and an act is unilaterally used to understand the same thing for the adolescent, an adult, a person in a long-term relationship, a person in a very short-term relationship, a person who has just had a baby, a person with many little children and an older person. How does this make good sense for an act that is affected differently every time our emotions, and both the external and the internal environments around us change?

The holistic wiring for each situation and phase in our life is a different one. Through all of our life's changing colours, sex and its implied expectations remain the same. This creates an enormous amount of pressure to perform, to match up to, and to desperately try to recreate the same result for immense pleasure each time. The worldly accepted standards presented for having sex are based on performance standards for procreating. Hard-ons and turn-ons are limited to physical functions. If we were not meant to procreate our entire lives, why would we expect our bodies to function in the same limited way for the entirety of our lived life?

Alternatively, pleasure, outside of limited physical performance, is limitless and its energy is available to all who continue to seek it. Pleasure can be discovered in the most simple of acts: eating a meal of natural, quality ingredients, reading a book that awakens the soul in agreement, the unexpected caress of a cool breeze on a hot day, a piece of art that stirs your emotions, connecting smiles with people, touching and being touched by people whose communication ignites sparks within you, and so many more possibilities.

Genuine pleasure is neither forced nor bought. Sensual pleasure needs to be discovered. It cannot be taken by force or for granted. Its outcome is like a new surprise. It is never uniform or specifically ordered.

In choosing to *Live Older*, I intend to remove or to walk around unnecessary illusory obstacles that are placed as barriers to seeking pleasure; mythical barriers placed by the opinions and experiences of others to limit my pleasures in life but which can be consciously removed from my path. In the time of *Living Older*, our awareness is heightened. It is the perfect time for sharing, feeling and touching within different forms of relationships, including a desire to be in the quality company with Self when desired. The most important requirements include sensuality, creativity, pleasure, respect and undiscovered possibilities. When we choose to be alive, our senses are on a natural high.

Resexatate™ for Partners

Follow guidelines and ideas created exclusively by the participants.

Create a space of mutual enjoyment.

Make no room for competition or measurements of any kind.

Follow guidelines and ideas created exclusively by the participants.

Allow rules to change when required so as not to allow for monotony—ever.

Eat food and drink that give you energy, rather than which depletes energy from you.

Be highly creative. Get the mind involved in play that comes with being in this type of environment.

Allow the spirit to be involved too.

Take time. Take all the time you need. Prepare for an event not just for the show.

Bring along the facility to laugh at your Self. Allow your chosen partner to laugh at you, if necessary.

Explore and play with no expectations.

Be respectful to all that is different from who you are.

Be in gratitude.

Be fully present.

Turn on all the switches of your senses.

Resexatate™ for Self

Know that you have every right to sensual pleasure.

Pressure in having a partner to provide pleasure is not yours unless you accept it to be.

It is much better with the right person that it is with the wrong one.

There is no limit to your imagination.

Wear Self-Confidence.

Eat food and drink that give you energy, rather that which depletes energy from you.

Bring all senses to the scene.

The only expectations are your own.

Being with a good partner is a gift.

Being with the wrong partner is a choice you can live without.

There are good reasons for inbuilt ways to providing pleasure for Self.

Never underestimate time spent in your own company.

Resexatate™ Imagine it. Start a conversation about it. Play with it.

Turn on all the senses for the carnival of pleasure.

15.
A Celebrated Life. A Continuing Journey

When we die, the chapter of our current life ends.

Whether a new one begins or not ... who really knows? The practice in not spending time wondering what will happen next allows for more energy to live life daily—now.

In *Living Older*, acknowledge that when we die, life for everyone else continues. Our loved ones and the people we may have touched continue to safeguard the memories of our love for them, the relationships we created, the good work we have done for others and the stories we leave behind, not the stories created for ourselves but the ones we created for others and left behind for them.

Imagine yourself at the very end of this physical journey. Would your final thoughts, if any, be related to a past, the present or the irrelevant future? What importance would these thoughts serve for you in your final hour? Death of a physical life has a compulsory completion in the journey of a beautiful life.

A non-disclosure of the actual timing of death, in terms of when it will happen, is a requirement for every living being. There are no exceptions.

We know this to be true, so why then do we live our present life in a race to accumulate material goods and to participate in competitive actions? Why is it that we renew, time and time again, the tendency to forget that death is not only for the old? Why do we forget that death can take any life at anytime? Why do we not choose as a priority to increase conscious value in preparation for the final outcome of our life? Why do we not live according to the standards we set for it without further procrastination?

Whatever the unknown number of years in our lives, the choice for how we live it needs to be a daily consideration. The primal Self needs food and drink to survive and it has the innate ability to inform us of this lack. Our soul is in awareness of its residence, in a physical and mental body, which is unique and complicated in chemistry, and is not invincible. It never was. It never will be.

Conversations concerning death are closed for many. Death, although a natural part of life, is not included in the daily contemplations of the way we live our material life. Alternatively, it is shrouded with taboos and negative airs. Instead, we readily place our entire lives in the whirlwind unconsciousness of material accumulation for goods and things we know cannot accompany us when we die.

When the focus moves away from the race of excess material pursuits, you begin to notice that every minute of life made available is a blessing. Each day brings a new opportunity to learn the existence of your awesomeness, measured not in the physical bits and pieces of your possessions, but in the magical exchange of your interactions with another. Such opportunities bring about the pleasure we experience in being in new places, and in learning to widen our minds, and in stretching the Self to the highest of highs. Great pleasure is brought about in learning the lessons of practice related to our connectedness with each other, and to all the other living beings on this planet.

Imagine, you are a car driving down the road of life and your vision is always on the rear view mirror, where you can live in the memory and in comparison of your youth that has been lived. Here, you can hold on to the belief that the more material wealth you own the better your life will be, until you crash your car and die. Alternatively, you can choose to keep your vision forward in full view of where life is taking you. You are allowed the enjoyment in appreciating all that is in your immediate Now because your vision is with you, and when the time comes to 'park your Self', you are ready to leave it in awe of the journey you took by owning what you are given.

We have the ability to reduce the focus on the greatness of our individual assets both in the competitive fields of physical looks and in cash accumulation. It all comes down to the power of individual choice. In *Living Older*, new standards are created to redefine the meaning of a celebrated life.

A celebrated life is neither about disguise nor about hiding and deception.

It is not about comparison because there are no twos of us. It is not about denial because you lived. It is not about fear because you need courage and perseverance in living a life that is owned and occupied. A celebrated life is not about competition nor is it about what age is a better ideal because each phase in the years of life brings a unique experience that is incomparable to the other.

A celebrated life is not about me, myself and I. It is about the number of souls, abiding in earthly physical bodies recognised and touched by the living of your life. Meanwhile, as your journey in life continues, the expiry date of your life is not a concern when you have so much good to do right now in its present moments.

Lighten your load by discarding useless thoughts that render no service to you, and be the star in the show of your life.

The Final Hour

A Sprinkle of
Last Thoughts

Oh! No more thrills for me.

This is the last time...

All these greedy people only want my material wealth.

I am scared about what will happen next because I was not a very good person.

What can I take with me there so that I am guaranteed the same comforts I had here?

Cheers to the beautiful life that I have had the honour to live! Here is to the next part of this awesome journey, whatever it brings!

Every new day I have received has been a gift to create another purposeful story.

My soul is dancing and my quiet conversations with it are as comforting as always.

What would you be thinking?

Celebrations for a Continuous Life

A Confetti of Ideas and Thoughts

Celebrations are more than a birthday cake or getting drunk.

Celebrate every new story that is created in *Living Older.*

Celebrate "Aha" moments. Many insights are only starting to make a deeper sense now.

Celebrate good health. Learn and teach to be in health, not to be in disease.

Celebrate the experience of pure joy and contentment in making the life of another living being a better one.

Celebrate the unique beauty of every age in life. No one age is better than another in a rich and complete life.

Celebrate silence. The ability to wilfully cut off unnecessary noise from your being.

Celebrate not knowing. Be proud of saying, 'I do not know, and it does not matter that I do not know'.

Celebrate the ability to love your Self.

Celebrate the return of the Elder. It will bring a more balanced evolution within the human life cycle. It will represent what a life can look like when it is lived up to its highest Self. It will also represent the values of a communal society, within which resides a variety of worthy humans.

Celebrate life by celebrating death.

The Mental

I know
because I seek information.
I love
because I read
what it meant.
I am turned on
because I am.
I gather memories.
Stored value
in a collection
of files and snapshots.
Should I forget,
Maybe it is best.
Should I forget,
Maybe it is best.
Should I remember
May be it is forever.
Switch on!
Ah! I see you.
Switch off!
Oh! I am lost.

16.
The Value Of Your Experiences Can Not Be Under-Estimated

You have only one life.

Who has the power to decide its value? It is an easy question to ask, but a hard one to answer. The noisier our world gets with pedlars pushing their sensual wares, the further away we get from our higher conscious centre. However, your conscious centre is the best place to come back and restart again whenever you are lost.

Our living environment is designed to entice us to always want something we do not actually need. This includes clothes, music, books, education, transport, as well as the search for someone you do not actually need in your life. **The Noise** is so well tuned that even in sleep, it plays like a lullaby.

This noise has stealthily changed the lyrics of our belief systems to those in favour of the ones with an insatiable hunger for more accumulated wealth. It is designed to numb our subconscious, making it easier to manipulate our minds into believing what we need to believe for a profitable benefit of another. Liking something is no longer a matter of an individual's thought when it becomes normal behaviour to ask for a 'Like' for a product or a service. The consumer as an individual becomes easier to manage via insistence and bribes by enticing freebies in exchange for being trapped under psychological means of subtly enforced influence.

When did we begin to believe The Noise for profit with such earnest intent? When did it become acceptable to take to heart undercurrent messages designed to negatively influence us with sounds and images that have no human relationship with us?

It is possible that it is impossible to tell another how to live their life.

Unconscious custodians of the planet cannot be told that they are a part of its quick destruction. There is an urgent need for a downpour of enlightenment to bring back to consciousness our state of numbness. We start with one person—the Self.

Humans are beautiful and complicated beings. On the one hand, we are capable of such big horrors, and on the other hand, capable of such soul-touching beauty. There are no preset tabs for who will be bad and who will be good. We all share the experiences in being happy and in being sad, in good times and in bad times.

The inability to be strong and in control of our lives all the time allows us to experience the roller coaster of a very colourful life, a journey far from monotony. The gift of the extended years of life is accompanied by an innate power and more time to get our act right. How can we refuse this gift by not living with consciousness?

When we shut down our consciousness, we allow ourselves to become numb and switched off. We readily give permission to others to take over our lives.

In *Living Older*, our past exists in the stories that we tell. Our actual presence has no place in the past. Of most importance is what is done right now. Our choices up until this time have been determined by the values of ourselves in the past, but our choices in living from this moment on will determine the value we create for ourselves in the very near future. In order to be of value, place your Self in the leadership role in living your true life-purpose. You are the sole driver of your life.

In *Living Older*, do not be in favour of segregation according to age. Each individual can flourish and extend its Self through the entirety of one's life journey. There is no predetermined benchmark for what is considered to be of value versus what is not considered to be of value. Value of Self is a private affair. Its definition is allowed to change through the many pit stops we make in our life journey. The expiry date of joyful experiences is determined only by the limitations of the person holding its value, not by its age.

In *Living Older*, do not stop the evaluation of Self. Look and see with different eyes, gather a polished consciousness, make more mistakes as you move into new areas, build more opportunities to create stories. As human beings, we seek approval. However, in the absence of consciousness, we readily accept all the subtle external messages telling us that we are not good enough to lead our thoughts.

There is a reason why drunken driving is dangerous. We are driving a moving vehicle in a state of intoxication of the senses and our cognitive abilities. Is it not the same when we 'drive' our lives in numbness? We become numb and quickly lose Self-value; it is the fading light of our consciousness that we have to illuminate. Its light and its strength will give us the calm, a quiet we need to spend in reflection and the time required to create a shield to protect us from the intruding noise.

Consciousness is the connection to the driving force, of why you are here. It is what allows us to have the simplest of pleasures at heightened levels. It is the source of energy we need to plug into when our batteries are getting weak.

A true value of Self cannot be bought or valued by someone other than your Self, unless you and only you choose to give it away to someone else.

Such is the nature of the value of Self. It is a priceless honour by which we abide, which in turns gives us the confidence we require to stay true to ourselves when the grounds of our foundations tremble.

In *Living Older*, the value of our age is not in proclaiming ourselves to be better than others or in knowing more than another. Our true value comes with recurring actions to be the best that we can be, as a loud example of quiet strength. The value of our age augments when the Self can take responsibility for the storytelling quality and the purpose of the continuous life it will live. The expiry date of such a life extends far into the vastness of the soul and beyond the physical limitations of a body that is its earthly residence.

Try *Living Older*. No excuses.

Leading Self

Make No Excuses. Try it.

1. Start by taking back ownership of Self. This is a lifetime endeavour.

2. Create standards for Self in order to clarify what it is you want from your life.

3. Initiate the spreading of kindness as a practice, starting with Self.

4. Listen to the people you place closest to you. They may know more about experiencing you than you will ever be able to do by yourself.

5. Learn to consciously create silence. Be comfortable in its presence.

6. Begin to understand the colourful spices of your vast emotions as a human being and how these affect you.

7. Allow yourself the flexibility of contradiction. The kind that comes with constant learning, the one that allows a woman to be a great leader as well as the best Mom in the world and the one that allows a man to be physically strong and to cry from a broken heart all at the same time.

8. Try to live and to progress without the need to label everything or to cage it.

9. Live the many colours of your life.

10. Go forth in consciousness without certainty. Rely on your inner wisdom to be your flexibility compass.

17.
What Do I know Today That I Did Not Know Yesterday?

The word 'older' brings along with it the notion of existing for a long time

This nuance of 'a long time' can have both a positive and a negative implic-ation. Positively, 'older' brings a wealth of different experiences in life adventures where not many have ventured. It is accompanied by lots of learning and energy of openness for the unknown. Negatively, 'older' drags along habits and recurring experiences that have no lessons attached to them. These repeatedly represent a person for a continuous amount of time, perhaps even their entire lifetime. If a human life were created for the sole purpose of finding work to pay their bills for a never-ending cycle of material needs while creating massive profitability for another, it would make sense that an older Self is no longer of any important positive value.

The older person whose larger percentage of life was spent in the service of a job certainly has something to share in lessons. However, these have little value in a world where the external environment outside of the comfortable workspace is changing faster than ever. Meanwhile, this older person is lucky not to have passed away from boredom and monotony while remaining in the zone of comfort. If a human is expected to live conscientiously and purposefully during the course of their life journey, the challenge is big when one is immersed in the designs of the rat race.

Go out into the unknown and experience something that brings a smile to your face without trying too hard. Place yourself in elements of surprise. Seek this experience in multiplicity. There is no attraction in listening to an old joke that is repeated over and over. The initial, raw reaction to the joke is the catalyst that provides us with its lasting fun effect. In *Living Older*, you will learn to inspire others with the lessons you have learned in the unique journey of your life. Every time you venture outside of your comfort zone where the scenery is constantly changing, you will learn more lessons as your perspective begins to shift. You will learn to understand why the lessons we have known to be true yesterday likely no longer work today.

Affirmations for Positive Life Change Cycles:

I will acknowledge that I cannot be an expert at everything I learn.

I will learn to listen in silence.

I will acknowledge that learning does not require only my intellect.

I will learn to learn with my senses.

I will learn to live today the best way I can live it.

I will learn the necessity of my ignorance. I will learn to identify its origins - fear, a disconnection or a voluntary disregard.

I will learn to live in my mind and body with awareness of Self, not from the influence of another mind and body.

I will not walk in the laurels of my achievements from yesterday, unless they are of service to me today in contributing to the betterment of someone or something.

I will learn to talk less about what I want to do so that I will act on what I want to do faster.

I will increase my pool of 'life inspirers' to include everything and everyone who has a different perspective of life other than my own learning limitations. This community will include plants, animals, the ocean, the moon, the sun, people of differing languages and ways of being, and humans of all ages.

I will be grateful that I am alive now, that I may design my today based on what I have learned from yesterday, so that I may be more centred tomorrow.

I will be worthy of wisdom.

I will wear the cool silver-grey crown of an authentic life well lived on my head.

Wisdom happens when we earn the ability to translate the knowing to the doing

Wisdom is not limited to possessing knowledge. Its higher learning comes from the ability to convert knowledge to an act of 'better-ness'. The truth is, many older people are older and very experienced in the use of their ignorance. When the title of wisdom is automatically bestowed upon someone due to a number of their chronological years instead of their experiences in consciousness, it is considered malnourishing for the soul.

In *Living Older*, it is not enough to think you know everything. We will acknowledge the continuity in learning by living with courage. In this space, fear of making mistakes or fear of being embarrassed are not an option, instead the best lessons in learning will stem from such encounters in being in the unknown territories of life experience.

We will continue in slowly understanding that I am not the "I" of this Universe. We will begin to experience how we are all connected and not separated. The ignorance of one person can become the design of a community spreading wildfire on this planet when we have not learnt the power of awareness and consciousness that resides within each of us. When we *Live Older*, we cannot afford the superficial luxury of ignorance by falling back and choosing to be disconnected. It is the best time ever to immerse our Self in the wonderment of being alive.

The possibilities are limitless.

The turn-on is dynamite.

18.
How We Will Age Is The Outcome Of How We Will Live Now

There is a lot of emphasis on being 'Anti-Age', like it is a terrible thought to avoid at all costs.

This ridiculous belief system is like suggesting that to breathe is to be uncool! What was previously accepted to be true in this belief system is of no purpose today to the many lives with wild souls.

Associating 'anti' with our increased years is unjustifiably allowing a lifetime of consistent disappointment with Self. Show me anyone who is not growing older daily! The concept of anti-age encourages us to continue living in the past. It leads our present thoughts and ways of being to constantly look backwards instead of keeping us focused and looking forward to the honourable finale of our physical life.

It is time to shed any cobwebs that entangle us on our life journey created by spiders waiting to eat us for their selfish profits.

Have we accorded ourselves such embarrassing lives that we need to hide and 'lay low' as we grow older? Everything beautiful about us can rapidly reach its constantly present opposite. For example, being good can change to being bad instantly. Being bad can change to being good just as quickly. Being unhealthy can change to being healthy and being healthy can change to being unhealthy at any time. A present state is never permanent. If we take some time to reflect upon this we come to realise that life is exciting because we are gifted or cursed with choices all the time, the final outcomes of which are never really in our hands or our well-planned strategies. The buffet of various choices available to us will depend on the invested value of what we have lived, and will continue to live, in terms of mistakes and experiences in the constant unknown. Take for example, the act of eating a food that causes us discomfort. If we have consciousness and awareness in place, we will be conscious of the discomfort. Now we have a choice in interpreting this discomfort. This will depend on a previous experience by our mind and body in a similar situation from the past. If we choose to ignore the feeling of discomfort, we made this choice, albeit not the best one, in the presence of our awareness. Whatever happens next as a series of consequences leaves us ready to make a better choice faster. The result of our choices is a constantly rotating effect.

The new vision of what ageing could look like starts in childhood, in their relationship with their elders. The relationship continues into early adulthood when the elders can serve as mentors in the search for a life purpose, beyond financial gains and careers that place them at the START line on the path of lifetime monetary quests.

What would ageing look like if we made the choice to change our old habits at fifty? Is it too late to gain more awareness, new skills, a higher consciousness and continuing experiences? I believe this is all possible without being too difficult. Imagine what this fifty year old could do with thirty years of a collective new and purposeful experience arriving at eighty?

In *Living Older*, you have to be consciously aware of the choices in living that we are making right now, no matter the age number. The immediate dedication and commitment in practicing this way of life starts the chain reaction of change to take place. When you seek insurance premiums to invest in the 'what-if's', you are willing to pay for what you know may or may not happen. You are willing to invest in an idea that has a fifty percent chance of ever happening. You may not be paying cash for how we live right now, but its impact on the outcome of our tomorrow is life changing at anytime.

I have started to live consciously today for a better tomorrow. It does not look perfect because I am not looking for perfect.

I am looking to roll in the dirt of a life well lived.

I am here, present and ready. Are you joining me?

The Now

Areas of Focus

The present, in this space, has no age-defining limitation. Any limitations are self-evoked.

1. Breath.

2. Awareness of Self.

3. Body and the Mind. How the individual body and mind react to what they are fed holistically.

4. Voice of the individual Soul.

5. Presence.

6. Presence of Self in an environment of others.

7. Provide joy in another.

8. Love absolutely the work you are doing for daily sustenance.

9. Create possibilities for purposeful work. It is healthy for it to change in time.

10. Do silly things so that you can laugh at yourself.

11. Remind yourself that you are not in competition with Nature.

12. Be thoroughly exigent about the quality of the food and drink you consume.

13. Practice Silence. Hear your Soul in this noisy world.

14. Perform 'shoulder showers' - Roll your shoulders forwards and backwards and open up the chest by stretching them gently at least twice a day, a practice to encourage a state of acceptance and receiving.

15. Celebrate the mistakes you make while exploring new paths.

16. Light up your eyes with constant curiosity when you arrive in the space of the unknown.

19.
Plan For What Happens If You Lose Control Of Your Physical & Mental Self

Fear, an emotion that kicks in to get us to drop everything in order to survive, is a response of apprehension for the mind and body to protect itself.

There are so many things I fear. With the experience in *Living Older*, I notice that my fears naturally increase alongside of my curiosity. The more I am curious, the more ideas I fear. This makes good sense.

If I lived in a cave, I would only need to fear what is in this cave. Once I begin to study the cave, the fears slowly dissipate with my new knowledge and experience. I become ruler of the cave. I become an expert and an all-knowing being of the cave. Soon, I will become bored and I would wish to venture outside this cave. Fear keeps me company again, until I decide to take the first steps outside the cave to learn what there is to learn. If a dinosaur eats me, at least, I would have seen more than my cave. The fear of not knowing where our lives are headed swallows us up and we compensate by the consumption of material goods, and we strive for more material success, and other illusions. The automated exercise in constant hoarding may be providing us with a 'security blanket' as we train ourselves subconsciously to avoid conversations about death and the unknown.

If we could get off the hamster wheel for a second to catch a much needed, tree-sourced oxygenated breath, we may begin to comprehend that our larger life is designed in the unknown, it has always been and will continue to be this way. We may begin to understand that death is not to be feared because it is a natural, beautiful and a compulsory process in living a life. We need to replace this fear with a better understanding of our consciousness in choosing to make the most of this life.

It is indeed interesting how the description of our fears change according to how we choose to live our lives.

For instance, how many of us are truly aware and afraid of global warming? How many of us are truly afraid of the fact that we have destroyed so much of this beautiful planet? I know that although this matter affects me tremendously, I am not afraid enough. Like most of us, I am living in my little cave. How did it come to be that we are more afraid of not having enough money than we are afraid of destroying this planet?

In *Living Older*, you will choose to learn not to be afraid of your transitions as you complete the circle of life. There are plans that we are able to make today based on the knowledge we have attained as a larger community of people. These plans may or may not serve us when we no longer have the mental ability to comprehend or to analyse them. Together, we need to create like-minded communities that will include human beings who believe in the complete circle of life.

I am interested in moving purpose, wellbeing and health towards the value of taking responsibility of family, including parents. In so doing, the larger community benefits with the energetic circle of being cared for and in caring for another as we are designed to do. By life design today, we spend too much energy and love in the beginning of a life cycle. We have the ability to give our children more than they need. This creates a discrepancy when care and serious consideration are absent from older children as a balance in reciprocating unconditional love for their aged parents. This is an important consideration that has left our world in an imbalanced state in which some only provide care and love versus those who only receive care and love.

In *Living Older*, we will create spaces that allow for conversations regarding holistic care, where a living being's spirit is never considered expired and of no communal value as long as they are breathing. We will create alliances and a merging of minds with younger people who are just beginning to find their place on this planet as they seek inspiration for ways to lay forth their individual craft to humanity.

We will create a space for human beings who are not afraid of death and the unknown, a place where the respect of the soul is maintained by allowing it to become larger in the deteriorating physical body as it prepares to take off from the runway of life.

When we begin to include death as an integral part in the circle of life, we begin to lose our fear of the unknown. We will commence new habits to value the magic of this uncertainty. The life choices we make will begin to lose their huge aura of invincibility.

The Plan

A Sprinkle of Ideas to Include

Design communities of like-minded people who choose to *Live Older*.

Consider provisions for this community to look after any member who may lose their faculties before their ongoing journey.

Live with the Highest Standard of Care of Self.

Introduce a 'Cleanse of the Consciousness' while you live in the knowing of today.

The only certainty you have is the one you are living in the moment.

Learn that asking for assistance allows another human being to test the level of their humanity.

Learn to stop planning family and communities around materialistic summits and to include them in the learning of care and kindness.

Be open and receptive to love and care.

Be in an environment that honours *Living Older*. Create it if it does not exist.

Be with people who choose to remain 'Alive'.

Shed away neediness and lighten the soul.

Create joy for the spirit.

Do not stop feeling—ever.

Heighten sensuality.

20. Design How You Will Age Now

The meaning of life is mine to define — only me, the individual and the unique life that is mine can make the best decisions for Self, even if I make some wrong ones. I have no interest in its meaning to science, or the results of a study conducted by other people with a small group of people who do not represent every individual on earth. I cannot afford to be distracted from staying with my own centre, which is a holistic experiment in itself, lasting me a lifetime of study and self-experiments. Before I begin these studies, I have to understand and accept the complete circle of life because this is the living truth. I have to accept that there is no other illusion. I know that I am awesome but I also know that I am not invincible. When I am able to visualise the path of this journey in the present as it moves toward the unknown, I begin the experiences that will serve as personal research in designing my life. My work in researching Self comes to me with a lifetime contract and a guarantee that I will not lose this job unless I am no longer alive.

The design of my life will start with an analysis of what is no longer serving me. I will determine all the habits that are needy and of no important use other than in depleting my energy. I will determine habits I need to adopt urgently in order to upgrade my abilities by creating a powerful surge like rocket fuel. As I progress slowly in the dark, I am introduced to aspects of myself I never knew I had. I am convinced that although my body will change, my research in Self is always beginning new lessons it discovers all the time.

Start with loving Self. In this love of Self, you will be able to do wonders for yourself and the world you live in. You will see yourself loving where you have not dared to love before. In this design of *Living Older*, you will make your life a purposeful one for the people you love and for those you will continue to love. It will start with positive intention that will serve as a candle to light the dark and unknown path of your journey.

My life was never a liability. It will never be a liability. If I were to be disabled, I would continue to learn a new way of being. If I were to forget, those who have loved my soul will remind me. My objective is to live a purposeful life that is not about being perfect by anyone's standards, especially my own.

Affirmations in Designing How You Will Age:

I will continue to create more stories. This I will do by not getting too comfortable in the material life.

I will display creative live energy in all I do and in all I am.

I will be in silence when it is time for silence.

I will draw positive energy from all that is beautifully imperfect around me.

I will sing and dance and play the drums even if I have no likes and only dislikes.

In my design of life, I can visualise that I will be in love with life a lot of the time

I will seek to be moved so as to nourish my Self and soul with all that is human.

I will continue to be skilled so as to carry with me the ability to be useful and to be self-sufficient.

I will continue to be a new learner by going into areas that I have never ventured into before.

I will not carry one drop of regret. If I do carry some of its attractive bubbles, these will burst rapidly.

I will be reminded of humility because there will be markers placed in the entirety of my design of life.

I will make mistakes. This will ensure that I am still not perfect and that I never will be. I will learn to want and to need less material things.

I will learn to acquire more of what my consciousness needs.

I will listen to the messages my soul wants to hear and move away from information that makes my soul cringe.

I commit to *Living Older* and to completing an awesome life.

As I close the last physical chapters of my life, whenever that is, I will be light and ready to soar.

Design How to Live Older

A Sprinkle of Questions to Consider

Am I afraid of dying? Take this question for many long walks!

Is my strongest asset the physical looks of my youth?

Have I taken the time to understand how life operates?

Am I lacking energy constantly?

Do I need some kind of stimulant to get me going through the day?

Am I afraid to laugh in case I develop unwanted wrinkles?

Do I truly believe that I will continue to own all of my material wealth forever and ever?

Am I wealthy in relationships that are real? Are these relationships those I do not have to 'Follow' or 'Like' on social media? Do these relationships require high maintenance?

How important is it what others think of me?

Will I be able to leave the comforts of my current life to start a new one

from scratch all over again? And again?

Am I afraid of growing old? If yes, refer to evolver #3

Do I believe that creativity is limited to age?

Am I afraid of being weak and frail? If yes, refer to evolver #3

Am I afraid of being dis-eased? Refer to evolver #15

Is there an importance in learning to eat holistically?

Do I believe that growing older means that I will be sick and needy? Refer to evolver #17

How many 'negatively-inclined' myths concerning growing older have I accepted to be true?

Why is it that there are insufficient stories being reported about interesting older people? Is it largely because we hear more about illness, boredom, repetition, and lies when it comes to older people?

Why do we disguise our 'elder wisdom' by colouring hair to mask off greys, ironing wrinkles to have faces devoid of stories by nips and cuts? It is easy to sell the illusion of youth to those of us who believe that it is shameful to look elderly. Find out what you are missing quickly.

Why is it that being older by years sells as being in regret of the past, as if being young is the primary and sole objective in living an entire life? We hear stories of being children, stories of being in the twenties, followed by stories of careers or work and then kids and family.

Why is it that interesting life stories seem to reach a dead-end around this point?

21.
Learn
Learn
Learn

The generation leading the path towards 'the new elder' is unique in that it bridges times of enormous change.

On one side of our births there have been strife and wars, on the opposite side there is a fast track of progress towards a world of technology, rather than a progress in the human condition. We have played a major part in all kinds of music from rock 'n roll to pop and techno of the eighties, and the information technology we worship today was started by people who comprise this same generation.

We have been schooled on topics of non-real time relevance and it has not changed. We are vital players in the makings of the rapid changes in this world, including the beautiful, the ugly and even the nasty. We are central to the development of the Internet, and we get to experience the trials and errors in pushing forward towards new life-changing ideas.

This soon-to-be elder generation does not have the right to stop thinking, taking action or to stop being of purpose as long as we choose to remain alive while still living.

There are many new opportunities and many radical new ways of being that are appearing on the horizon. We have been a part of its creation, and we need to continue to proceed in processing all the possible outcomes—both the very good outcomes and the not so good ones. Care for the planet we live on is being disregarded. Its abuse is unprecedented due to our willing state of numbness and the lack of compassion in many human hearts.

We all need work to put food on the table but destroying the planet in the process is not a right we have. We need to create exciting new opportunities for different types of work to be available for our choice which supports our consciousness, brings out the best of our human spirit, and comes with flexibility, allowing for organic change and adaptation as life experiences flow in and out on the beaches of our lives. Our perception of being materially rich needs to be redefined as having abundance as our focus moves forward instead of backwards at our current destination in our life journey. The allure in the traditional ways of working as a little peg in a large machine is shifting more and more toward the individual of any age who craves the freedom of movement, and who needs to feel the wind of travel and change in their veins; an individual who can design a service or a product and offer it to a large number of people without being enclosed within any space and limitation.

Increasingly, even platforms for learning are becoming more and more creative and abundant in choice. There is a wealth of learning available to re-understand what we have learnt previously, but within a larger mind frame. The introduction of a new and different perspective at every transition in our lives allows us to go deeper into the depths of our understanding, providing us with possibilities to constantly upgrade our knowledge while evolving towards our better Self.

How do we define being old in the context of lifelong learning? It is the time when a person, at any point in their chronological age of reference, begins to narrow their personal space in the development of Self for the beneficial use of other living beings, including the planet. This truth is available for observation. Be clear, dear reader, I am not narrowing the context of learning to a subject in school or in the pursuit of higher education. I am focusing on the learning that comes from a commitment made from within the individual to gain diverse knowledge and to practice it for good use.

As long as you are equipped with the ability to learn and to develop the skill of adaptability, there is no stopping you from staying connected to the importance in making life an adventure, whatever the design.

Learning When Living Older

A Sprinkle of Consideration

1. See new opportunities for purposeful work that is waiting to be enlightened by your unique brand of passion.

2. Craft your own business. Stand outside of the rat race for a better vision of purposeful work tailored for you.

3. Be less fearful by planning a time for reflection.

4. Choose to centre your life in accumulating endless material goods or contribute to the value of Self to the others of this planet.

5. Experience what happens when you follow your passion instead of your fears.

6. Own your life. Respect and honour the different phases of your life's evolution rather than disguising or hiding it.

7. Understand how your mind and body works. Begin with awareness.

8. Believe that mistakes are acceptable. How else can we progress towards unchartered territories in living this beautiful life?

9. Be very adaptable with the attitudes you wear.

10. Know the difference in value between inspirational experiences versus the value of experience.

11. Be silent.

12. Every time you say, 'I am too old to...' you are narrowing down your opportunities with intention.

13. There are many ways to learn today, the downside of which is that there are too many. We can get stuck in a continuous learning mode that takes us farther away from a required action mode.

14. True value only starts to count when we use what we have learned to make life better for the larger living planet.

15. The global world has made it possible for us to learn any language, culture and particular way of being. Be invited by your consciousness to learn these new and challenging ways.

Learning When Living Older

Continued

16. Expand your mind with global knowledge. In practicing this, you will create an openness that will allow for more passion, kindness, and humility as you are rewarded with never-ending possibilities.

17. Being older does not automatically make you wiser. Being wise requires a love for constant learning starting with the learning of Self.

18. There are many ways to learn and there are many ways of being. There is no one right thing for everyone.

19. Honour the lessons left to us by past generations.

20. Nurture future generations to be the best that they can be. We need to learn how to redefine the value of communities who look out for each other.

21. Develop new ways in determining the meaning of success.

22. Redesign success away from the accumulation of material goods. Create a balance in Self that includes the consciousness.

23. Exchange the feelings of stress, expectations and rankings that come with learning for feelings of joy, exhilaration and individually translated possibilities.

24. Make money by sharing of your Self in doing what you feel connected to do most. Being good or doing good does not mean you cannot make money.

25. You are the unique gift that is inherent to your individuality. It is a power that is yours to keep or to give away. No one else is to blame. We come alone, we leave alone.

26. There is no time limit in learning. The only limits are the ones we place on ourselves.

27. It requires intelligence not to know everything.

28. Create more work that pleases wild souls.

29. Get excited.

This is the perfect time to learn, learn and relearn again.

A Side Story

I have had a continuous relationship with learning. It has a tendency to start with a keen interest in wanting to learn something that is led by an intuitive attraction towards learning it. A matter of financing this learning usually becomes a problem that goes hand in hand with the powerful desire to learn. I then get confused, worried, and panic because the excited emotion to learn something new is so compelling. When this pattern starts to manifest itself, I have learned to focus more on reflection in quiet time while I connect to the centre of my consciousness.

Two years ago, I finally signed up and was accepted for a doctoral program. There had never been a doubt or a worry in my mind that I would lack the ability to complete it. I wanted to make a difference and I had found my path within education, not schooling education but the kind that would change the way we operate, and the kind that would provide a methodology to push boundaries towards more and more opportunities where we have not tread before as human beings capable of learning.

I started my programme with lots of excitement as I began to visualise where the end of this learning would take me. After three months, I slowly began to understand this learning was not about taking action towards change, it was largely about following on the footsteps of many who had trod the pavements of talking and analysing change with lots of writing about it. I scored high in critical thinking mostly because I truly was connected in wanting to create what was needed to make it happen, not only for those who could read and write but also for all others who are confused and living in a world that is changing too quickly.

As two more months passed, I began to feel every cell in my body 'screaming in pain' as I prepared to reference more and more papers. I came to understand first hand, why certain people became disillusioned with the academic platform.

At the end of seven months, I decided to put the doctoral programme on hold and eventually did not go back to it.

My decision opened up other doors for my specific wants and needs. It was only a matter of time; after all, my objective in the exact learning I needed never wavered.

More importantly, I learned to place myself in a situation I dreamed was the best one for me, I had my consciousness available as my compass and I learned to remove myself from what did not work for me without regret, remorse or an extra look backwards. I have learned and experienced so much more in making the decision that was true for me, while I was in the dark about what consequences my decision would carry with it. The fear and the adrenaline rush turned on their sirens, not to scare me, but to warn me that I was about to go into unknown territory, again.

These and many more lessons like this one are the biggest and most rewarding lessons to be found on life's journey.

If your eyes only see the highway, it is impossible to describe the immense pleasure and unexpected gems that can be found on the scenic, smaller routes where so many more unexpected opportunities lie.

22. Calculate The Worthiness Of Your Life

How I Could Grow Older

A Readily Available Possibility in Living an Ordinary Life Today

1.

Birth

Schooling for the purpose of acquiring the possibility to earn money

Work for the purpose of making money

My wants and needs (this will shift according to my momentary emotions)

Spend money

= The Commercial Value of My Life*

*The Commercial Value of My Life is the measure of how much money and accumulated wealth I may or may not have in comparison to other human beings.

2.

The Commercial Value of My Life*

Do I have sufficient cash to maintain the cost of living a life?

= Retire from the Corporate World

Retire from Purpose or

Retire from Being Alive while Still Living

How I Will Live Older

Adopt these Elements
as a part of your Attitude
in Living Life

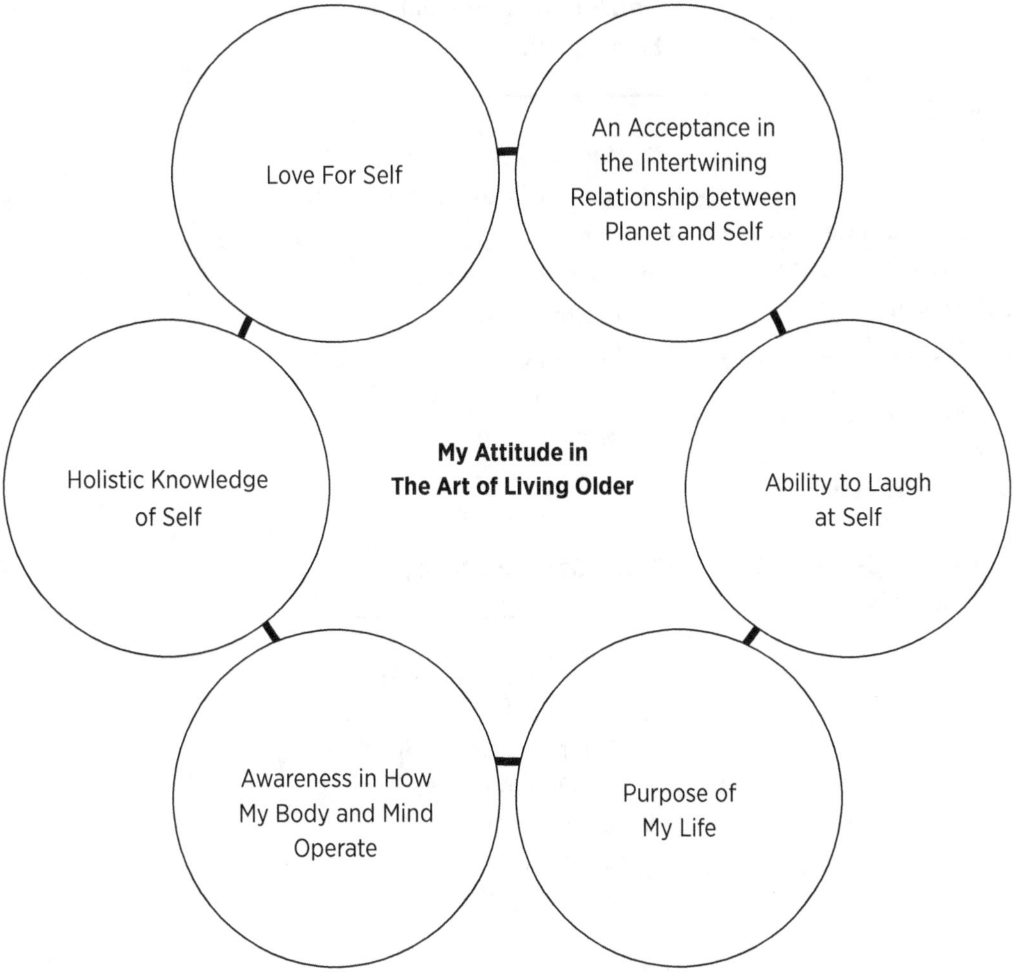

Love For Self

An Acceptance in
the Intertwining
Relationship between
Planet and Self

Holistic Knowledge
of Self

**My Attitude in
The Art of Living Older**

Ability to Laugh
at Self

Awareness in How
My Body and Mind
Operate

Purpose of
My Life

What I Need To Live Older

Skills to Do What I Love

1. Hands Skills
2. Mind Skills

My Inter-Connections with The Planet and Other Beings

1. Time Spent with The Planet
2. Time in Silence
3. An Ego Cleanse
4. Feel the Centre of My Consciousness

What I Will Do For Work And/or The Freedom To Live My Life

1. Money Earned
2. Money Invested In Self
3. Money Saved
4. Money Contributed To Others
5. Tax and Other Such Necessary Earthly Requirements

Tools Of Consistency

1. Embracing Transitions
2. Adaptability
3. Health Awareness Check
4. Learning from Mistakes
5. Good Fear that Comes From Doing Something New

The Worth of a Life in Living Older

An Equation in Living Older

1. My Attitude In The Art of Living Older

— A Narrow Mind

+ The Skills* to Do What I Love

— Self-Imposed Limitations

+ My Inter-Connections with The Planet and Other Beings

= **What I Will Do For Work and/or The Freedom To Live My Life**

↓

Money I will Attract Sufficiently for My Worldly Needs and Exchanges

* Must include both Hand skills and Mind Skills

2. **What I Will Do For Work and/or The Freedom To Live My Life**

x Tools Of Consistency

= **My Ability To Embrace The Unknown**

3. **My Ability To Embrace The Unknown**

÷ (Humility + A Connection with The Soul + The Universe)

= **The Worth of a Life in Living Older**

↓

The Outcome Of Living Older

23.
Invest
In The
Freedom
To Be
You

The Freedom to be 'You' requires three parts to show its true beauty:

1. Be fully present in any given moment.
2. Respect the free space of another being.
3. Maintain awareness.

Here are some examples - if you have awareness in feeding yourself today, you are investing in the freedom to be the best that you can be physically, mentally and emotionally. In creating and/or accepting the work you do today with your consciousness present, you are investing in a better sustainability for this work and in its results for tomorrow.

The concept of being an individual is not about being a solo act. When you are the best individual that you truly can be, you set out to clear the path for what you want to do in consideration of others, and what your presence could bring into their lives to make them better. This is far from an easy task, but in maintaining the high standards in knowing where you need to be it helps to make this an easier investment for your Self and your learning experiences in life.

The word investment here does not take on the term as used in a business where profit and loss is the only consideration. In this context, it concerns making decisions about what you want as an outcome of your completed life, not just life here in this physical world. Experiencing the true freedom to be your Self allows all of your life's purpose and vibrant energy to flow through you giving you the impression of flying. Like eating the right foods provided by Nature, it's a well-digested life where there is no constipation or fear. Be free to make mistakes and to celebrate them.

It is only in allowing your Self to make valuable mistakes as you venture into the new and the unknown that you may discover a better way of being.

In finally owning and embodying our Self, perhaps we will discover we were free all along, bound only by our own limitations that were created in fear, excuses and the warmth of comfort. Once we get the taste of whom we are meant to be, and we are able to live it, time and the changes it brings feel irrelevant.

A Side Story

There is a reason why one loves a certain kind of work while another hates it. There is a tendency to believe that we are limited by choices, while actually, we are surrounded with possibilities. The real problem is that it is difficult to reach these possibilities when we are looking for easy ways to make the right choice. We begin to notice that there are too many weeds, dark corners, and other unknown factors, while we fail to see all the beauty available in the smaller spaces that require us to look with focused care and intention.

When we are disconnected from a life purpose and choose to remain on the known and paved path, it is unjustifiable to feel unlucky when we do not feel good about where we find ourselves. In simpler terms, we took the easier choice, the one that allowed us to avoid the difficult action we needed to take in order to gain the deeper wisdom of our innate conscious communication.

At the end of a well-lived life that is anchored to an intuitive guidance, the sense of pleasure, gratitude and perfect connection to all that is beautiful in life is truly priceless. No one can remove this from you, no one, but you.

24. Money. Redefine Its Value

There are many more ways to generate earnings of cash other than being employed; however, courage and a sense of adventure are required.

Applied practice will allow us to not fear money or to worship it as the ultimate possession in answer to all of our problems. When there is a hindrance in cash flow, it could serve as an opportunity for you to shine the bright light of your imagination. It may provide you with time to unleash creative energy, or time to learn the necessary survival skills.

We cannot continue to believe that lots of money only equals bad things, either. Our level of consciousness is separate in importance to the quantity of money we own.

When good walks away from money as a tool for the game of 'world meets consciousness', we leave lots of money in the hands of those with ill intentions to abuse others and the planet.

Good people need to make money and to remain good people.

Conscious moneymaking is not restricted to age. In *Living Older*, we will define creative ways to earn positive money and sustenance all through the valid phases of the life cycle. The word retirement is used to explain the end of a job or work done for many years, possibly a lifetime, but it does not stipulate that living stops.

Money serves as a tool of exchange for things we need in *Living Older* – a solid investment in Self, good health as an assurance to be the best of our ability, and a positive attitude as an inbuilt design feature.

As for entrepreneurs, the excitement of creating supply for demand far exceeds a numbered age. Entrepreneurship is an art form when it is designed to do more than make cash. The excitement begins when you notice challenges, possibilities, and opportunities only you can see, causing your mind to be in doubt, triggering showers of fear for your senses to remind you that it has no familiarity about what you are going to do next. This is when the fun begins.

Explore and determine your exchange of service for cash. If no one is offering you purposeful work, create it yourself as an entrepreneur. There are many people waiting to work with you in shared values and gratitude.

There is an urgent need for good people to create money for good.

Oh! The Many Languages of Money

Haunting Questions

1. How much is enough?

2. What is the price of freedom from the rat race?

3. How much less money would I need if I buy half of what I am buying today, most of what I do not need?

4. Am I rich in cash and virtual investments but poor in soul-searching?

5. Am I poor in useful and exchangeable skills for trade?

6. Am I living my entire life to work for money?

7. Am I living my entire life to spend money buying material things that lose their initial value immediately after the purchase is made?

8. Is the fear around my life without money a real one or an illusive one?

9. What if I run out of money? It must be better for me to stay employed in a job that enslaves my life just so that I do not have to fear lacking money.

10. Is my work status my ticket to the best life after death?

The Energy of Money

Positive Reminders

1. Money is a tool that will allow good to take place.

2. It is not money that is the root of evil; money is a tool that all evil knows how to use.

3. Good people may be running away from money thinking it is evil.

4. Money responds to energy. You decide if it is good or bad.

The Environment

I control you
or you control me?
I need you
or you need me?
I affect you
or you affect me?
I feel different
when you change.

My good.
My bad.
You have
Influence.
I take from you what I need
to live.
My breath.
My life.

25.
Be
Alone
With
The Planet

Our minds are cluttered with expectations, worries, messages, questions, outcomes of our choices in relationships with others, and a whole lot more. Conscious PAUSE and EJECT buttons are required, albeit temporarily, to walk away from the clutter and The Noise and into a space of aloneness, not loneliness. Just you, yourself and the Universe, out under the large embrace of the vast open sky. This is a space where we can connect to the 'WIFI' of the trees, the winds and Nature as they communicate a type of busy, versatile, communication in potent silence.

The ability to be alone in this space provides a gift of immense balance with your core centre—a connection of ourselves with what is to be, and a connection of Self with the larger forces out there, the ones that understand intuitively that we come into this planet alone and will depart it gloriously alone. We leave in our stead an energy of our presence in memories from a life well lived so that others may have hope in living theirs even better.

In cities, we give accolades to man-made creations, and we are left in awe with some incredible accomplishments. We move in rhythm with our overcrowded minds that are overflowing with a million things to do in any one day. We forget the daily canvas of artwork on the natural sky as day turns to night and night to day. We fail to observe, like our consciousness, the impact in the energy of the changing moon and the interpretation of its cycles.

These are communication systems that have been left for us since the beginning of time. It is a media of communication we mostly ignore as taller and taller buildings fill the skyline. This is not an invitation relevant only for those who live in cities, it is extended also to people in the country who may have started to take for granted this powerful gift at their doorsteps, or for those who have been well informed to choose what they know to be home.

When you begin to understand that Nature is designed to nurture you with food, oxygen and healing energies, you may start the process in really saving the planet.

The anger that exists in this world that stems from the disconnect we all face leaves us behaving like spoilt brats who constantly want attention for Self, with no time to share in the plight of other beings, including the planet.

The **Phuckploration** of the planet is an expression Nature might create as an accusation about human behaviour if it could express itself with the anger it would feels towards our actions.

In *Living Older*, we practice the embodiment of our actions to the tune of the planet. We practice a conscious responsibility towards the planet and all of its inhabitants who do not partake in the massive accumulation of money strategies. It is a time for us to understand how the choice in what we buy and whom we support is a pro or a con to the planet.

Biodiversity, our interdependence and the ways of Nature are lessons readily provided by Nature when we take the time to visit her in silence. Connect to the 'WI-FI' of Nature's healing energy. Turn on the device of your inner consciousness, much like the silent and majestic trees as they remain true to their grand purpose while surrounded by many other trees, different from one another. Each tree is endowed with the innate wisdom of their connection in purpose with each other.

Discover yourself and realise that all of your issues are really small in this vast and opulent spaciousness. To be in silence with the planet requires us not to talk. There is no requirement in articulation or explanation. There is no need to impress. There is only room for awe. The sole requirement for connection with the planet is to be in its silence. The silence eventually translates into a connection with the multitude of languages expressed by the many citizens of the planet who communicate in harmony one with the other.

Here, we remain in silence, learning to connect with our humility as we are reminded of the usefulness in both the grand and the minuscule. It is a reminder that no one operates alone, and that everything has an important purpose.

In the silence, you will understand that you share this planet with other citizens to whom have been given no rights, as they have been shut out or shot down. There is no demand for an app that translates their language of a cry for help, or their questions about our relationship of interdependence in the accord of maintaining life on this planet we are designed to share.

So many of our co-inhabitants on this planet have not been accorded any rights to democracy. We have quietly annihilated them in the noise of our daily search for a quick fix and in the multiple seconds of numbing pleasure and never-ceasing demand for more and more material things.

In seeking to be alone with Nature and the planet, we learn many valuable lessons. By not talking in the language of humans and in being present in silence, we will be allowed to comprehend the language of the planet. A language fast becoming extinct as we evolve far away from being the custodians of this infinite balance that sustains us with no sense of monetary gain.

In being alone with the planet, you connect with your life purpose despite the mental absence in logical thought. No matter your beliefs, religion, spiritual teaching or way of being, you share this powerful place to heal from the weariness of the material world. Here, you observe the value of life and the respect in death. In choosing to spend more time alone with the planet, you will quickly reconnect with your internal consciousness where you may find the answers to assisting the planet, in healing it, too.

The understanding of such power does not require a firm, broken down and fully analysed explanation and proof. Trees from springtime move beautifully and usefully through the other seasons into winter. When autumn drops its leaves on the soil, the leaves serve a purpose in preparing for the new spring, covering the soil as mulch. Although the leaves have dropped, the tree stands strong, not useless or forgotten. It remains a part of the natural cycle of life.

The mystery of how Nature operates in its extraordinary facility is key to the idea of this connection. The proof is in the bliss you feel as you smile for no reason other than feeling connected to your soul.

How to Plug-in to The 'Wi-Fi' of Nature

1. Find a spot outside in Nature.

2. Be grounded with both feet touching the ground.

3. Put both arms out to your sides, palms faced upwards towards the sky.

4. Your spine feels in line with the ground.

5. Feel the spine supple, not tight. Relax the muscles around the spine.

6. Imagine light shining through the spine.

7. Keep eyes closed and relaxed, or open, but relaxed with Nature.

8. Breathe. Inhale slowly and naturally without making it too technical.

9. Feel as though roots are growing out of your feet into the ground.

10. Create and connect yourself with the earth and its elements.

11. Be aware of all you feel and sense.

12. When you start to feel like everything around you is starting to narrow in too much, (desperation, questions, frustrations and such) go outside!

13. Be in the larger world with Nature. Watch and observe.

14. Feel your soul do the celebration dance.

15. Fuel up on this Energy.

16. Get high on it.

Connecting with The Planet in Manners Out-of-the-Ordinary

While waiting for a train on the way to work or back, put on earphones or headphones to shut off other noises and virtually transport your mind and soul to your favourite place within the natural forces.

Walk, even in the dense city. Feel the air on your skin and find the time to look up at the sky. Remove your suffocating shoes and allow your feet to feel the earth.

Find your little space to be alone with the planet. It is time to be in your presence with stillness and silence.

Learn the importance of the moon. Look for it and connect its energy to yours.

Rise with the sun and start to rest as the sun is setting. If this is quite impossible, be in its awareness so that you can endeavour to redesign your life around it.

Dance with your soul at every opportunity.

26. Share Crafted Food With Many People

We all know that food is a necessity for life.

As we get busier and busier, our feeding patterns and our food preparation abilities are becoming less and less exigent. As long as it tastes good and it is not costly, the idea of eating as soon as it is possible becomes more and more pleasing. If we were able to put our lives in slow motion for just enough time to connect with our innate need to feed with pleasure, we would realise very quickly that experiencing sensual eating is one of the best pleasures in being human.

Do not get me wrong. I am not talking about foods that are enhanced with artificial flavourings and additives to please the senses in your mouth alone. I am referring to foods that have been crafted as you would a loving gift made from your heart, hands and blessed with your soul. The work in preparing soulful food holds magical secrets that are difficult to decode. Its art lies in the contagious effects of the good vibes it is able to spread.

Looking for quality ingredients that are grown by Nature's strict ecological standards is a necessary part of this journey to crafting good food. However, it does not mean only foods that are expensive or exclusively for profit. I am talking about foods that are real and designed with all the complexities Nature intended.

Real food is as real as an honest person.

It is vital for the experience in the journey of soulful food to know the story of the ingredients you are choosing to make your 'piece of offering'. This story starts with the birth of the ingredient. Who was there? Where was it? How was it cared for before it became available to us?

Identifying quality is a variable dependent on the openness of the information we have and the personal choice that comes into play. In the developed world, there is plenty of choice in food. The ratio between the quality of real food ingredients available and the multiple options of replacement processed and convenience foods is determined largely by the choices made by the people of any given community, both in their feeding rituals and in the importance of the community's wellbeing. A tour of the local market, supermarket or a farmer's market can indicate the consciousness level of who lives there.

It is important to question whether our choice is made with the wide knowledge of our individual awareness in body, mind and soul, or within the narrowness of its absence. The preparation of food is an art form. You can take a recipe, available to all in the many cookbooks out there and on the Internet, and follow it in minute detail but the outcome will be different one from another because of sheer and wholesome magic! The energy that was available in its preparation becomes a vital part of who we become after the consumption of the meal.

When we use ingredients that have been locked up or mistreated, there is a possibility that we are consuming emitted energies of fear, mistrust and pain. Food can be a true feast for the senses. Or it can be the opposite. Everyone can cook. Everyone can learn many different methods of cooking. Competition in the preparation of food is like claiming that there is only one best art piece on this entire planet.

Food designed with the priority resting on satisfying the tongue, the eyes and the brain is readily available and an objective that is easily accomplished. It is one of the reasons why processed foods are accepted easily without a thought.

Working with crafted food, on the other hand, is like dancing with a rebel. Once you get connected to the groove, you are drawn into a sensual world like no other. Each new dance becomes an entirely new experience.

Crafting food from Nature's source keeps you humble and in awe of a creation that is bigger than any number of years of experience or knowledge. You have to learn to connect with it. You need time to learn its communication. Like Nature, what the Source produces has many unknown and unexpected outcomes. This is the magic I want you to create and experience! Our senses never know what to expect from the start to the end of its preparation.

The craft begins at the Source—the origin of the ingredients (not the country of origin but its actual birthplace). The stories centre round its conception and the intangible reactions the ingredients have to their immediate environment and to their care or the lack of it. These are not the stories that are drawn up by suits playing with words, using illusive tricks on our minds so as to create personal profit. As humans, we are continuing a process that was conceived by the forces of Nature when we use what she provides for us. Learn to cook. There is a lifetime quantity of technical knowledge and experience that can be acquired. Learn to relax in its preparation. Remove all expectations and conditions. The celebration of food is a vital need for all living beings. It is also one of the most useful artistic creations that we can offer as gifts to each other.

Preparing crafted food for sharing is a lesson in itself because it is, by its nature, already difficult to cook a great meal for one person. There is always extra food. Crafted food made with intent and good energy has healing and comforting abilities that will provide a heartfelt satisfaction every time. The importance in consuming quality-sourced foods precedes any other quest in living. Sharing food with others allows us the ability to spread a vital little gift of our time, love and energy to people we know and love from our entire lifetime, and to others we are just getting to know. There will always be people ready and in need of a little human connection.

Add a dash of inspirational conversation, a squeeze of laughter, a canopy of stars, music that soothes the ears, and we are rejuvenated and deeply connected.

If we are alone, preparing crafted food allows us to share a celebration of love for ourselves, an extension that provides the ability to forward the extra morsels from our table to others who may need it, perhaps for other 'alone people'.

In *Living Older*, we will continue to create many more opportunities to be a part of crafting food. From the origins of food sourcing, all the way to coming up with creative and different ways to share such foods with others of differing needs, enables us to move the attention from Self to another, commencing a chain reaction that sparks passion and lust for the sensual and beautiful life.

The Passion for Food and How It Would Not Go Away

I was trained for hotel and restaurant management in Switzerland. I got there as a matter of geographical convenience rather than actual choice in a career. Medicine was my first option at the time. Many such unintended outcomes became the best directions for my life to move into the future of unknowns.

I started training as a chef at age eighteen, and I loved the work but did not enjoy the actual cooking at all. At this point, it is really too early to understand your true Self. The right things can seem wrong and the wrong things can seem right. Alternatively, the right things can seem right and the wrong things can seem wrong. I was lucky because I had a strong tendency to follow my gut feelings. I was never lazy but I did have strong intuitive impulsions that I followed without much logical thought or elaborate understanding.

At the time, I learned what was required of me to learn, but with no enjoyment for cooking. So, I pursued management options in restaurants rather than the cooking ones for the next few years. There was no mistaking my love for people and a confirmation to have fallen into the best work for my way of being at the time.

It is only thirteen years ago that I began to look at food as I do people and other living things. I began to understand the interestingly complex characteristics of food as living things, or at least as originating from living things. I began to experience their immense healing powers. In so doing, I discovered the multiple energies of their beings as I would the many different people I was encountering.

This time I fell in love with food. It was not love at first sight. It was like suddenly coming to a realisation that you were always deeply in love with an incredible best friend who was always there. I just was not ready to see it. When I was ready, the feelings were immediately very profound and deep.

My newfound attraction to food was no longer about just eating. It became centred in the entire experience around the food that I would choose to prepare. It was necessary that I was available in its presence. I needed to be present in all of the details of its preparation. It was almost as if it transported me to its inner world where the food and I were now in tango from source to preparation, and from cooking to the eating experience.

The consumption of food is an ultimate event for me and for the company I invite. I do not cook this way very often. On a daily basis, I cook to feed and to eat with the same energies with an ultimate celebration of life.

There is nothing that matches a feast for the senses as much as a meal cooked with great energy and shared with many.

27.
Share The Outcomes Of Your Mistakes: The Good The Bad And The Ugly

The art of storytelling is enhanced by a good story.

Extended years in age provide a library of possible stories that will overshadow the competition. Good stories are true experiences in living, not anecdotes that are copied and pasted; they have their blood running through your veins. There is a difference between telling a story and sharing an experience. We all undoubtedly have a collective number of both to share.

In *Living Older*, we need to become very comfortable with our experiences. In the temple of social progress, our vast multicultural, multivariable and multi-coloured ways of being in this world have been narrowed to 'Like' and 'Dislike'. With so many words in a dictionary—even a very poor one—we can describe the many variations of any individual experience in life, but all of these are ignored. The two word options will determine current social opinion within which your story or experience needs to fit. The words are then placed in the powerful hands of so many people you have never actually met or know about.

On social media, if you are 'Liked', you might receive a noisy fanfare for what you did or said. If you are not 'Liked', you will possibly be verbally abused by those who presume the right to do so. Either way, the jury on this one is usually hiding behind a device from which they make comments about other people's lives. Imagine going down the road, actually finding real people, looking at them in the eye and soliciting them to 'Like' you or to 'Dislike' you for what you have to say. Hmmm . . .

We are a part of a system that celebrates the illusion of a non-existent singular perfection.

What is pretty and good looking is embraced without much thought. If there is 'some ugly' hidden behind it, then it is feasted upon with detrimental comments. In *Living Older*, we have to create real opportunities for sharing our mistakes. We need to put a focus on the life we are living as designed by ourselves, not by the specifications given to you by the many ordinary people around us.

The life we design has to include a provision for mistakes. It cannot omit the bad and the ugly. How else will we fathom the balance required in being better people? How else will we learn to be with compassion for other individuals as they work on designing their experiences? If we live our lives driven by the fear of being judged for all that we choose to do, are we truly the owners of our lives?

Designing our personal pathways and journeys requires that we own this life. In its ownership, we will invite humility. We will have crafted a well-earned way of being. In choosing to *Live Older*, it is necessary to share the outcomes of our lives with all of its many honest and vibrant colours. Standing on the top of a high mountain shouting out our claim to a fantastic experience is not as mighty as standing firm and still in inspiration. True inspiration comes from the truth. It is magnetic to those who are in need of it. In *Living Older*, you will have a continuous lifetime worth of experiences to share.

The stories of your childhood and earlier years are only repeated for a limited time for others. The experiences you seek every day in your living life will provide a reason for you—the principle character in your life—to be solely responsible for the stories you create. The stories you create are not always yours to tell.

Perhaps the best of your stories are the ones you never have to tell, but the ones you pass onto others to live and tell.

28.
Do Not Let Others Decide How To Measure Your Life

One of the most liberating experiences we will learn in *Living Older* is that as humans, we have a natural tendency to stray from a path easily and very often. We set out to live a certain way with goals and objectives, we become very focused and clear in what we want for ourselves, then Bam! We are hit by a passing comment someone (a loved one or not so loved one, and even a no one) will make about us. We face the consequences of these painful and confusing comments with emotional upheaval and turmoil, and we may start to feel like we are sinking into a quicksand of self-doubt. Only a little while before, we were certain this quicksand was removed from our constant search for perfection.

To *Live Older,* we must accept that you will fall and you will hurt and you will mess up. As a matter of fact, it is the reality you must face in order to obtain experiences that count.

More importantly, we need to have an understanding that being in a quicksand of self-doubt is a required challenge that must be overcome in order to experience the affirmation of our strength and love of Self against the judgements of others who will come our way in the journey of life. It takes a lifetime of learning to not live in the pretence of perfection. It also takes a lifetime of learning to understand that it is not our life's work to change or to correct the actions of other individuals. We require a lifetime of learning to master quicker ways out of the life-sucking quicksand.

In *Living Older*, you will choose to strengthen the individual Self. It is only normal that you are sometimes standing on new, shaky ground that you are testing to best suit your current evolution. This shaky ground can represent the good, the bad or the ugly while you are trying the best one on for a perfect fit.

Practice to become more stable in your choice and decide how much power of Self you will choose to give away to others. You must begin to observe that when you do not love yourself, there are others for whom their life's work is preying on your self-hatred. They will smell the scent and come quickly to take advantage of your self-doubting opportunity. In adopting this understanding, hold yourself up with pride as you stand for the meaning of who you are, even if just for a moment. Multiply these moments by *Living Older* now!

My Selfish Life

As the numbers of my life increased,
I learned to be selfish.
Selfish not in the inability to share a smile
to someone who looked sad.
Selfish not in the inability to assist
to offer my hand to help.
Selfish not in the inability to love
Whole heartedly and not afraid of pain.
Selfish not in the inability
to offer my shoulder of strength for a weary head
Selfish.
Very selfish.
In choosing the design of my life.
There is only one I have.
The life that is mine
to make or to break.
Since, no regret was to keep me company
On my journey of living
This life I lived.
Selfish.

29.
Spend Time Alone. Get To Know Yourself By Your Self

We do not have to be alone to be lonely.

We can choose to be surrounded by family, friends, colleagues and even lovers, but still feel terribly lonely. However, we do need to be alone to be alone. Within whatever context, time spent being alone requires a conscious choice. It is often a misconception that time spent being alone must be boring, scary and, let us face it, kind of sad and sorry. In certain circles, someone 'being alone' is even considered weird and the person considered a loser.

In order to escape such labels, we surround ourselves with groups of vacant people and overwhelm our thoughts with noise. We can choose to keep 'alone' company with our ears closed to the beat of music playing from our earphones or headphones. There is nothing wrong with listening to music depending on the answer to the question: Are we listening to music because it is soul enriching, or are we allowing its noise to block out the thought of being alone and not liking it?

I can feel the sticky claws that take a hold of me and weaken my resolve to let go of whatever it is that is keeping me from spending alone quiet time with my Self.

In being alone with your Self, you create an opportunity of silence to listen to what your soul is telling you. Being alone illuminates your consciousness. It invites you to get to know your demons, your fairies and maybe even your long forgotten invisible friends. It allows you to listen to the very subtle music within your souls.

For those of us who have been in the constant company of relationships, family, and friends, choosing to be alone is a scary feat. Fear is reminding us we have acquired a safety attachment preventing us from doing something important that we need to face, and have instead, chosen to avoid. It does not mean that we have to be always alone, but it does mean that we need to value time alone as an important time for Self. We are able to listen to our souls in our time alone.

Upon being alone with myself, demons may come visiting, dreams may become clear and reality may have a chance to show its true colours. Whatever the outcome, I need to sit down with them and be in their company in order to know who I really am, and if I like who I see.

This is a scary experience for many of us in our times of poor choices. Blocking the silence is an easy way to avoid this important conversation.

It is a conscious time spent away from blindly following the music of advertisements and the constant information of the Pied Piper filling our ears both subtly and **bombardistically**!

Take time alone slowly—one moment at a time. Get to know your Self, alone in the company of Nature's powers. Start loving quality and silent time alone.

Loneliness and aloneness could be twins, except one would be needy, the other free.

Self Alone With Self

The New Social Allowance

1. A time to confirm that you are all right.

2. Touch base with yourself.

3. Realise how you stand up by yourself when you go out into the world.

4. Display your Self as an exhibit for 'people watching'. This will create an opportunity to stir your primal instincts for self-recognition.

5. Appreciate people who are constantly around you when you get back to them.

6. Test your capability in being good company.

7. Time spent alone consciously is not the same as when your ears are 'plugged-in' or you are hidden behind a book.

8. Be alone outside in the world. This includes watching other people, observing yourself, listening to your thoughts and the music that plays in your mind. Use this time to be aware of thoughts that preoccupy you in times of 'busy-ness' as well as thoughts that have not yet had time for quality reflection.

9. Invest this time to be friends with your Self.

10. Be away from the judgments of others.

11. Test your fears. Test if they are true or false fears and determine what you can do about them.

12. Practice listening for peace and strength in being alone.

13. Find strength that will fuel the energy required to give of your Self to others you love and the people you want around you. Communicating with millions of people within noisy media platforms is not the same as communicating with ten real people in silence.

14. A time to cultivate humility.

15. A time for deep reflection about the resumé you have created for the life you have lived.

16. A valuable time to keep your ego in check and to not allow it to fly off like a balloon out of control with no purposeful direction.

Creating 'Alone' Time

No Matter the Circumstances

1. Listen to your own intuition for what the Self feels like doing in the allotted alone time.

2. Plan for alone time, in advance. Allow for no interruptions.

3. Alternatively, be impulsive and do not plan alone time. The impulsive act comes with more vibrant energy.

4. Express your 'aloneness' with attitude, in dress, in style, in your unique 'swagger' or in the feel of the moment. Celebrate the occasion in silence.

5. Place yourself as an **aloner** in areas filled with other people. You do not need to alienate yourself into a quiet, dark room for alone time.

6. Choose to be alone with Nature. The 'WIFI' here is free and it provides ample energy to the Self that you need to live your best life.

7. Choose to sit, be stationary, or move constantly while being alone, as in a walk.

8. Allow thoughts, feelings, and emotions to be open, without forcing yourself to analyse them. Just be with them.

9. Welcome your demons or negative thoughts for company. Try to understand them, why they are there and find out how long they intend to stay.

10. Welcome your friends, the positive thoughts. Ask them if they can come back more often.

11. Welcome back your invisible friend, the one from your childhood, to stay for a while.

12. Experience that you are never truly alone.

13. Get in touch with awareness.

14. It is all right to have a different experience every alone time.

15. Implement for at least fifteen minutes, once or twice in a day, to be alone with Self. Use this time consciously with nature, in meditation, in prayer or whatever suits you personally, to assist in keeping you centred.

30.
Know Your Centre. Come Back To It When You Stray

The coconut tree is one of my favourite trees, amongst many other favourite trees, including all the trees in the world. It's rooted deep with a flexible trunk and branches that reach out far; when the wind blows they stretch out even further as they dance to its rhythm. Then it comes back to its sturdy centre when the wind passes. I like to imagine that I am living life like the coconut tree. In *Living Older*, we must adopt the idea that our exceptional individual energies are best used on changing Self rather than in choosing to change others. In a life journey that continues, learning opportunities are never ending. Getting side-tracked by letting other people affect our lives, and then blaming them for the consequences, presents a perfect opportunity to review our ability to come back to our centre.

Check on awareness. Does it keep you company or do you have to consciously invite it to come stay with you? I need awareness to be with me so that I can feel the feelings I know to feel. I need it to remind me to know what I already know but perhaps forgot. It is the premier gift within myself that guides me back to my centre.

My centre will ring the bells of my consciousness loudly for not complying with my set values of Self. It will allow me to be serious and to experiment, while keeping me from going beyond my set values. It gives me the possibility to develop my personal perspective on my Self—my actions or non-actions, my environment, the acknowledgement of other beings around me, and a whole lot of light or darkness within and around me that is constantly revolving. I practice one of the visual examples in the following pages to assist me in removing all the negative and damaging energy, effects, thoughts and actions from my Self.

In *Living Older*, you consciously redesign the way you live to allow for being lost. In history, no change for the better was achieved on a well-paved path. Actually, the more you get lost the more you are provided with an opportunity to check the Self, including its abilities, and strengths. The act of being lost confirms that you are not staying in the glorification of your comfort zones, and reminds you that you dared to move further than you thought was ever possible. More importantly, we can be secure in the knowledge that as far as we may stray, like a boat venturing into a stormy sea, our centre is like a lighthouse shining its light of consciousness to guide our return.

Centring

A Necessary Practice

1. Spend at least two to three times a day being quiet for ten to twenty minutes.

2. Use this time to connect deeply with your guiding centre or your core.

3. This time is available to practice awareness in thought and in action.

4. It is a time to touch base with your humility so that ego remains tamed.

5. It is time available for deep conversations with the soul.

6. Get in touch with your feelings and your emotions. Take the time to sort out what serves you, and remove what does not serve you.

Affirmations for the Centring Practice:

1. I am allowed to make the new mistakes I need to make as I journey into the darkness of the unknown, slowly in search of lights I need to switch on. It allows me time to correct myself in consciousness, regularly avoiding the accumulation of unnecessary weight.

2. I allow enough time for me to see that my problems are not attached to me. I become aware that I am able to discard these unnecessary and illusive problems, they can be separated from me.

3. I can continue to make choices about what I do next with this burden.

4. I can continue living with the new life lessons I learned.

Benefits from the Centring Practice:

1. The availability of a reset button.

2. Overpowering burdens can be visually moved away from the consciousness of your being.

The centre is where my consciousness resides. My soul plays here a lot.

Connecting With My Centre

Creating Opportunities

1. Practice this: Stand on your two feet. Feel them carry your physical weight. Close your eyes. Keep your head straight and facing ahead. Try to stay balanced on your two feet without starting to sway. Feel the muscles of you body work together to hold your skeleton up. Bring in positive and nurturing thoughts and inhale consciously. Remove damaging thoughts from your body through conscious exhalation.

2. Take your Self for a walk in the company of Nature.

3. Dance with the consciousness of your Breath.

4. Proactively make little changes. For example, greet someone whose gaze, even a momentary one, connects yours during a walk, at work or at a market. Make the first move. Do not let the crucial moment pass. This practice has led me to experience people who do not respond. It has also led me to people who have responded with the biggest lit-up faces of smiles that have made my day richer. You get used to it for the bigger blessings.

5. Stay authentic to who you are as an individual.

6. Celebrate who you are, not the person someone else would have you believe you need to be.

31.
Be With People Who Light You Up

Throughout this writing, the idea of celebrating the individual is in context with being the best individual human being that one can be. As individuals, we all have both similar and unique choices in life. When we live with an intention to celebrate life, numerous conflicts of interest appear.

Like individual paintings using the same primary colours for multiple levels of awesome pieces of work, there is no one exact experience in life.

How and what you choose for your life is effectively what makes you an individual. When you look at life this way, there actually are no limitations. Some of you may have to climb higher mountains and cross through deeper valleys, but nothing can stop you. Some of you need to remain in the deeper valleys so that you can nurture others who must climb higher mountains.

Appropriately, we may not really know who we are or how we may react to circumstances until we actually are face to face with them. In choosing to *Live Older*, we begin lessons in awareness of our dance with these different and unknown challenges. We become aware of our reactions and we begin to create the possibility of reflecting on them during our times of silence.

A permanent existential truth is that, outside of our Self, other beings are constantly in a dance of their own actions or choices. Whether these beings are the closest people we love; our parents, our children, our life partners; or whether they are people we relate to daily at school, at work, our friends and acquaintances; we do not want to spend our vital energy in trying to manipulate their choices in the path that is their life journey. This is not our life's work. It is not a human right to control the makings of another individual's life path no matter who we are. Re-channelling this vital energy towards change of Self is much more efficient and deeply rewarding.

As we all rotate around our own vortex of life's journeys, we are placed in contact with people who are not of the same frequency in our circle of relationships. Temporarily, we are carried away by someone else's dreams and objectives or we choose to stay far away to avoid feeling pain. Either decision will be an experience to try out our imperfections and to start a new story.

At times, when you are more positive in outlook towards your challenges in your life journey, it repels you to be in the company of people who have chosen to take on a more negative outlook toward their challenges in the life journey. This makes chemical sense because we are not attracted to what repels us. Some of the symptoms in this situation include a feeling of being pulled downwards, an unlikeable heaviness in your Self, energy that starts to feel like it is being zapped out of you, unnecessary complaints and feelings of misery 'gate crashing' into your being through contagious infection.

If this state of being serves you, even momentarily, and you are aware of your choices, you will be fine. If, however, you are quickly losing control of your own awareness and energy, it is time to press the EJECT button and pull your Self out of this powerful negative environment. When your state of being begins to be affected by other people's current state of negative mind, it is a very good indication to walk the other way.

Problems, issues and challenges have their share in the ingredients of the necessary cake we eat in the journey of life. They contribute to the vibrant and non-monotonous beauty of life experiences.

In order to experience a great life, you need to include relationships and opportunities to connect with other living beings. Added to this skill is the ability to implement a choice of who you want to remain while you are connected to another being in their life journey.

When we are with people who light us up, we feel exhilarated. A magic spark is created that keeps us interested, spreading energy we want to adopt. Inspiration becomes easier. Laughter becomes natural. Our soul feels a natural high that it shares like rapid fire with the body and mind.

The privilege of being with people who light us up generates inspiration to become people who will light up others in a contagious connection of positivity.

Whether the connection lasts a second or an eternity, there is no space for consideration when basking in the momentous high we are experiencing in the present now. The feeling we get in being lit up by pop stars, rock stars, sports stars and movie stars is not what I am talking about here. Being in the spotlight literally creates more artificial light shining your way, which creates an unfair comparison. I am placing one human being with another on equal footing on the stage of life where there is no wealth comparison or work comparison. There are only soul connections, where equal beings are making the most of their lives.

In *Living Older*, you will continue to learn how you are able to light up yourself first. You will start with an awareness of your limitations and weaknesses, as well as your strengths and your scope of abilities gathered from your experiences.

When we continue the practice of lighting up our own lights, our souls will provide the glow from deep inside. There will be no mistaking its recognition by other souls, both the brightly lit ones, as well as lost souls who are guided to shore like ships by a lighthouse.

Soul Greetings

A Sprinkle of Ideas to Try When Walking

1. When you are walking down a street, keep your face looking straightforward. Chest opened and shoulders relaxed and held downwards.

2. Hold an invisible smile on your face. This may sound like an unreasonable task but it is worth the practice.

3. People you encounter will either interlock their eyes with you for a very brief moment or they will not. If you are listening to your intuition, you will know when not to look at the person opposite you, too.

4. If there is a connection of a fleeting gaze, the other person will break into a smile as they cross your path on the street.

5. You will feel very good because your free WIFI was available and of high frequency.

32.
Hoarding.
Be Heavy
Or Be Light

Space around us both private and public is inundated with images and sounds, real and unreal, strategically placed to subtly bombard us with messages to buy, buy and buy.

The messages play with our insecurities of need and of never being good enough as a simple and extraordinary Self. If we choose to follow through with these powerful messages encouraging us to acquire things, we will live our entire lives believing we never will be good enough the way we already are.

After all, why would you want to be the complex 'You' of unique calling when the superficial world is designed to make it easier for you to fit into a ready made box that is already cut out for your life purpose – service to others who need you for their personal profits? Consumerism is an easy means to lose control of Self. Some lessons are readily available for us in watching those who spend their entire lives accumulating wealth, only to leave it all behind when their life's expiration is due and a ticket for extending life could not be bought. (Refer to evolver #22 *Calculating The Worthiness of Your Life.*)

The design of our individual life choices will determine whether we will be swept into the tsunami of a hoarding culture. We all need money and enough skills to barter for what we need in the system of exchange created and accepted by us in the operating system of our world. More importantly, we need to live our soul's purpose.

In *Living Older*, we accept death as very much a part of life. We know to be true that it is not limited to being older. In accepting this living truth, we continue to learn that our needs required to live well in this world are actually very simple.

Our world has so much to offer in terms of beautiful art, travel, food, and craftsmanship. We need to encourage and to contribute to such work by being a part of its conscious consumption. There is a positive need for cash in order to spend it on exciting your senses with what you like on social media, if what you 'Like' is promoting a 'viral' culture of healthy sustenance, support, fair trade and pro-Nature choices with other individuals who have stories and yearnings just as we do.

Whatever the number of material assets we have, it does not determine if someone has a better valued life, just as the number of years one has does not determine that one has a better life than another.

To *Live Older*, turn on the light of consciousness when you make your purchases. Support a purchase that is made by hand to last so that it can be enjoyed and valued for a long time without converting to unwanted and purposeless toxic garbage for the earth. Take a good, close look at what material wealth you have accumulated, and the time you spent throughout your life fearfully protecting what someone else may take away from you. Ask yourself a personal question, are you a hostage to this accumulation, or are you free because you lack it?

When we design our lives around the wealth of experiences rather than material goods, there is an immense sense of satisfaction. For some of us there is value in travel because it connects us with people and ways of being that are different (with choices, not the soul) from us, who provide us with opportunities to craft our skill as offerings. The exhilarating experiences add to our accumulated wealth in the journey of life. It is true; however, that this way of living may not be an ideal choice for all of us.

The best way to travel is with as little material goods as possible. The extra space and lightness gained will be used by the soul for priceless connections, communications and experiences that will last a lifetime and perhaps longer in the memories of the inspired living.

With awareness, we will realise quickly how many unneeded things we have accumulated. The switch in choice for living lighter provides a wealth of space free of material things in exchange for the intangible weight in experiences that become a part of our Self, not luggage we carry or wheel on the side.

If being surrounded with material wealth is making you feel heavy, trapped and lethargic, it may be time to free your Self from it. This will allow more space for lightness in consciousness and spirit by opening up possibilities for simple, fun experiences, with no prerequisite of having a certain quantity of money available.

Hoarding is also applied to feelings, emotions and experiences that do not serve us any longer. By discarding them, we will gain more space to add other consciously chosen experiences, such as acts of kindness, which are very light to carry and serve as a good medium for barter. Being kind to other people requires that we put in place some solid self-awareness measures to not be deceived by those who prey on good and kind people.

In the adventure we call life, living and travelling light allows us to remember there is nothing more we can take in death other than the soul with which we came.

How We Earn Cash and How We Spend Cash

Vital Questions in Determining Distinctions

1. Did I earn this cash from the hard work of my mind, hands and creative spirit?

2. Did I sell my soul in order to earn it?

3. Am I making a purchase based on the subtle humming of the **Buy-Buy-Buy World** and the loud banging of 'Be someone else'?

4. Who are the beneficiaries of the money I paid for my item? What is their story? How will my purchase serve to make their life a better one?

5. Why do I need it so bad? Am I sad and feeling low? Is the purchase giving me a distorted gratification?

6. What is the domino effect of my involvement in this purchase?

7. Does it match my consciousness?

8 Did my purchase have a positive effect or a negative effect on the living planet that has no say in its treatment? Our planet is literally filled with our unwanted impulsive purchases. Yet, the planet has no say in the matter of what we are throwing back to it.

9. What will I do with this purchase when I no longer need it? A purchase made in the presence of awareness requires more time in thought about its value.

33.
Take
Time To
Give
Of Your
Presence

If there is only one of you, then you must be extraordinary. Now go find at least one other extraordinary to share your life.

Soul conversations require no interpretations. Instead, they reward us with the easy choice of being lighter in material acquisitions and heavier in the experiences and skills that are required for positive change; including, laughter, simplicity and an exchange of stories. There must be importance in human connection. Why else would we have charm, the ability to love and to hate, and the ability to communicate in so many ways?

We possess an innate ability to be repelled when a possible human connection does not suit us. Of course, sometimes our judgment for another person can be impaired; however, when the chemistry of attraction is present, it is accompanied by a priceless feeling for the validation of our uniqueness by someone else. A sense of conscious fulfilment is acknowledged to be important for a human being. The connections are not limited only to immediate family, friends, and acquaintances. It is strongest when we push ourselves to include a 'wide lens' of others whom, like us, live choices, have struggles, and whose ways of being have similar needs and challenges. A unique Self provides relief for someone else who is in need of the remedy of its presence and its connection. When this interaction happens naturally, it is accompanied by a simple, yet potent validation for the value of a person, which is far deeper than the quest for accumulated wealth.

To create a presence, it is necessary to be comfortable in your very own skin, which houses your soul. It does not require you to comply with standards pronounced by another person. Shining the warm light of your unique presence is a deep form of communication in the darkness of navigating through rough terrain in the journey of life. It is like an inviting inn located in the middle of a long trip, a place where one can rest their weary soul and collect memories of connections with other people before continuing on the path of their unique life. In *Living Older*, choose to be available for a story. Share with another generously of your unique presence, in silence and with your voice.

The Walk of Life

My soul, my body, my mind and I
went for a walk today.
A strong wind blew
body lost step.
Down on the ground
we laughed
My soul and I.
Body is bruised.
Mind is upset.
But soul and I
we laughed.
We lifted them up
and gave them a hug.
My soul, my body, my mind and I
went for a walk today.
A strong wind blew
In front of us
person fell
Down on the ground.
We helped him up
His eyes met ours
His smile was ours.
My soul, my body, my mind and I
We laughed.
My soul, my body, my mind and I
went for a walk today.

How To Spread Light

A Sprinkle of Initiations

1. Laugh out loud so others in your presence are affected by its contagious nature.

2. Admit your mistakes, no matter the number of your years.

3. Buy a sandwich and give it to someone who is homeless, if you believe that a gift of cash may be abused by the purchase of unsavoury things.

4. Convert the limitation of excuses into endless opportunities.

5. Adapt the volume of your presence according to the situation. If your presence is overpowering, it will repel another. Remember too much light can blind.

6. Make the first move to assist or to connect when you believe in something that is happening in your presence.

7. Be in the company of your soul as much as possible.

The Spirit

As Light as you are
within me.
I feel you
in the depth
of my core.
You keep me rooted
as my wings
span wide.
My ego,
My pride
will stay humble
with you as my guide.
Lessons,
You teach me
are simple
but oh! So big in practice.
My north you remain,
as I tread
on unknown terrain.
Stay.
Because you are the
Me,
I need to be.

34.
Move
The Body
To Its Own
Rhythm

Music, no matter the genre, is great therapy for the soul. Not to be excluded is the original music that creatively plays in your own head. The larger the variety, the more there is to appreciate and to enjoy; however, all the rhythms of music we hear may not be attractive to us when we are forced to analyse their effect on our minds, rather than our souls. Of most importance is what music does to us at a subconscious level.

Our bodies hold a lot of constraints in our physical Self. Our cultures, our societies, our parents, our age, our sexual or nonsexual status, and our nature of work have a lot of influence on how we carry our physical selves. When allowed to dance, we put our bodies on a pedestal for criticism about how we move or how we do not move. We believe there must be a perfect way of movement in which we must excel to be allowed the pleasures derived from the movement of the body.

The simple truth is that moving the body to its own rhythm allows for any individual to take part in self-pleasure. It is the ability we have to move aside the mental overloads we carry and to celebrate being in sync with our souls. One of the best highs we can achieve is the one obtained from moving our bodies to a rhythm it translates as unique unto itself.

A dance that comes from allowing the body to move like a magnet in rhythm to its interpretation of the music it hears is choreographed by the soul.

Moving our bodies in absolute freedom to its own rhythm is incredibly liberating. It assists in altering our sad moods and in channelling creativity. If nothing else, rhythm simply allows the body to move. The soul can now come alive to feel its essence in the beauty of life. There is a secret communication between music and the way the body naturally interprets rhythm. Subtle differences in the way the body and the mind are feeling at any given time will lead to the exact music someone is seeking.

Movement is necessary. On a vital and a superficial level, it confirms to us that we are in ownership of our bodies. It reminds us that we can laugh at ourselves.

Creative movement is healing for the soul. In order for my body and my mind to function, I need to dance freely. The flow of energy it releases in the eyes, the digestive system, the blood, the mind, and the emotions, fuels the motor for my operations as I journey in life. The opposite of the experience would feel like living in a body and mind that is required to function in putrefied, stagnant water that becomes smelly and absent of any life and energy.

Movement and Strength: Stretching and free movements in rhythm assist in removing the spider web visuals beginning to accumulate internally within the stagnant stance of your body and its operating abilities. The energy that results from such action will provide you with a drive to smile, to laugh, to build our strength and to carry on.

Movement and Awareness: The ease in moving to the rhythm of your music reflects how comfortable you are within your body. It also allows you to understand why we may not be so comfortable. Are we worried about being perceived as silly? If yes, what is wrong with that? Why can you not be perceived as silly? Why is someone's judgment of you so important to your individuality? In gaining understanding, we can begin to evolve.

If you require intoxicating your senses before you can let your Self go to the music, it is possibly a reflection on how many burdens you carry by the judgments against your individuality. This represents the need to artificially lighten your burdens before letting your Self go to the music. Moving your body to its own rhythm allows you to become more familiar with the internal communications it is having with the Self. Is your heart beating too rapidly? What did you put into your body and mind today to create this effect?

What type of music beckons you? Is it always the same music, or does the music vary according to how you may be feeling? Is there a need for an audience? The scene is yours to set. A variety of options are always available with plenty of room for more creativity.

What matters most is what the soul is feeling as rhythm and movement bring together your mind and soul in a union of gratitude and celebration for the life you are living at any moment.

How To Embrace A Feeling Of Silliness In Movement

Dancing in Squares

1. Draw squares. The size is up to you, your mood and creativity. Alternatively, find a floor with geometrical patterns.

2. Turn on some music or play a tune in your head.

3. Move according to your intuition using the points of your feet to move from square to square.

4. Move according to the beat of the moment.

5. Play with others or play alone.

Chair Dance

1. Move any part of your body to the tune playing in your own head.

2. Depending on your chosen variation, you can do this by actually moving any part and every part of your body and mind without getting up.

3. If the chair has wheels, you are in for a wheeling blast!

Dancing Inside Myself

1. Best used when you are feeling down, sleepy or not physically and mentally present in a situation that you cannot get away from immediately.

2. In your head, play your favourite tune or create your own according to the environment of your mood.

3. Watch a vision of yourself dancing to the music.

4. Feel the vibe of your reward.

5. No guarantees that you will not start moving!

The Strut Dance

1. When you are walking and not choosing to be in silence, walk each step in celebration of your life.

Warning: You may find it difficult to control your inner smile!

35.
Savour Each Breath That You Take

If my life has been a fun ride, it is because I designed it to be this way. I have made many mistakes and have no regrets. I have consciously accumulated many experiences and skills. Yet, it is only very recently that I learned the importance of the breath; I have only recently relearned how to breathe correctly.

How can this be real? Is it not what you need to learn first and foremost? We all know that in order to live, we need to breathe. We breathe. When we are not silently listening to the rhythm of our breath, we begin to take it for granted as its precedence falls to the back of the list because of the everyday demands of our wants and needs.

I am not going to go into the mechanics of breathing here, I will leave that for a better opportunity in live sessions. What I do wish to share is my experience in the value of each breath and its importance in *Living Older*.

Savour each breath like a morsel of very well crafted food rather than gulping it down like low quality fast food.

In being conscious with each breath, take the time to notice how difficult it may be for you to take it slow. Begin to notice how conscious breathing affects the heartbeat by calming it down. Develop a realisation of the value of each breath. The consciousness of breath connects you back to the importance of Nature and how it quietly sustains you with her omnipresence.

Savour each breath like a morsel of well-crafted food.

When you feel like there are too many burdens on your shoulders, or when your fears starts to take over you, a valued breath can bring you back to your centre from where you are able to create better solutions for your troubled Self.

Lessons in the benefits of conscious breathing are profoundly valuable, without which we could not attain all else we require for the holistic journey in living a life.

I realise that old habits in breathing are difficult to correct. However, in itself, this is a lesson. Every day, I need to be reminded to practice it. Knowledge confirming that proper breathing is imperative to our well-being is one thing; learning to savour it slowly and consciously in order to experience its beauty and its effect is quite another. A savoured breath provides us with an opportunity to slow down, like a built-in stopwatch it enables us to consciously come back to the natural rhythm of the vital single breath.

It is a skill that requires a lifetime of learning.

Of course, it is!

Savour One Breath at a Time

1. Choose the best available environment for you, preferably in Nature.

2. Upon inhalation - visualise and accept with each breath all of the goodness in this world and the goodness within you.

3. Upon exhalation - dispose of all the negativity, bad feelings, and all that does not serve you. Be in gratitude as you become lighter in spirit, be grateful for the gift of the next new breath.

36.
Rewrite
The Recipes
Of How You
Act And
React

Do not book a ticket to the Land of Perfect Pursuit.

Au contraire, be alive and depart from the Land of Numbness. Explore the Capital of Encourage, a beautiful word in French meaning - to be surrounded with courage. To be encouraged is to live in the moment with courage, to accept all the different flavours of life as they become available to us. As the years of a life increase, our mind and body become more certain regarding what they like and dislike. These are filed as habits and their function becomes automated. The mind and body have cleverly assisted us in developing positive actions towards what we like, and not so honourable actions towards what we dislike. It's a good reminder of how we are able to work together as a team. However, life happens all the time, and the timing of a type of experience cannot be programmed in advance.

When we design our lives as if we have total control, certain experiences and their accompanying outcomes can be very disturbing and frustrating because they do not match the idealism of our life. However, the not-so-perfect timing of such experiences actually enriches our lives further. In the absence of consciousness and in the abundance of many apps to solve organisational problems, we become arrogant in believing we are in control of our lives. How dare life do this to me? Living within these chosen limitations for the Self leaves us broken, disappointed, angry and without love. In this environment, and without our conscious eyesight, we are unable to see a new path made available to us for a better adventure that must first be earned.

If you choose to wear a pair of 'consciousness glasses' over your myopic eyes, and pick up a suitcase of curiosity as you proceed on this new and very rough path, you will certainly fall. It is only natural to fall when your senses, your existing habits and your mind-sets have no experience in travelling this path. Yes, you will fall and you will make mistakes, and many more mistakes. It is time to get over it! Mistakes that turn out to be the right ones allow us to gain mastery to embrace our challenges, providing a quick upgrade to a life journey filled with adventures each unique and incomparable.

There is an art to making the right mistakes.

Mistakes are harder to live with than to talk about. As a chef, I chose to move away from my traditional training to something very personal and individually creative. The result of my decisions was sometimes terrible and with dire consequences. However, most of the time the result was incredibly satisfying and empowering. The only way I am better within my own capabilities is when I allow myself to embrace the bad tasting experiments as much as the outcomes that are terrific. Alternatively, it is much easier to perfect yourself by remaining within established comfort zones already perfected by someone else. Meanwhile, you can also accept all the second-hand glory you require in accolades and compliments. I am not stating that this way of being is wrong. Au contraire! I am acknowledging that although there are many life templates available to choose from, *Live Older* authentically with your life.

There is no better rush in creative energy than in the joy of making something from scratch that is truly your own.

I note, with interest, how the life I live has an effect on the way I prepare food. The energy of the environment, the people around me, and my state of being are intangible ingredients that make a very big difference to the required creative outcome.

When you operate from a place of awareness, by *Living Older*, you begin to understand and to see for your Self how you act and how you react to the events that unfold in your life. Some events come to you as a series of consequences from your previous actions; others come to you as a series of experiences you were meant to have. With awareness, you can accept where you are in the event as it unfolds. This provides for the best action, or lack of reaction, according to your present abilities. After the event has unfolded, you can reflect a little deeper in order to identify if there may have been a better way to act.

The practices of awareness and reflection will happen as a natural process that will be implemented by Self to keep you open to learning from mistakes, and to cultivate courage. They will work as a team to remind you to keep your head up high by owning your actions. They will assist you in achieving a feeling of lightness and in creating baggage-less possibilities as you move forward deeper and deeper into the journey of life. Your soul will dance in body and in mind as it readies for the next experience and challenge that will come your way. For all of this to happen, you must accept that awareness and reflection can be your constant companions.

Enjoy the moments of life's challenges. Feel the blood running in the arteries as you confirm that life is indeed still within you. Retrieve the power of your existence, a priceless force, which is purposefully designed within several seasons. Alternatively, it will be easy to buy into the illusion that being old means you are useless and in yearning for the spotlight of your youth, as if youth were the sole purpose of your entire life.

What you have to present on the stage of your life performance does not require noise, bright lights, theatrical makeup or costumes. The empowering presence of your soul as it becomes larger in a morphing physical body is all that is necessary to steal the show.

Turn on your spotlight, there is no need for someone else to do it for you. Take time to rewrite the recipes of how you act and react. Be the best you are here to be. Discard what no longer serves you.

In time, the recipe of your life in action will take on a rich and delicate flavour, smoothly textured and perfectly crisp in the corners, providing a satiated sense of pleasure and fulfilment.

37.
Reinvent Self or Celebrate Self For Who It Is

Two options are available on the menu of change - Reinventing Self and Celebrating Self.

To reinvent Self, you have to acknowledge that change for the better is an option that is constantly available. Reinvention takes place no matter our age, because it is never too early or too late to change the Self at any given moment. Some limitations exist, and they will always exist, but age is not one of them. Self-imposed limitations are the biggest limitations. Daily practice in becoming expert excuse-makers is another big limitation. A better, alternative practice is cultivating our relationship with consciousness.

The first lesson to learn before reinventing Self is how to own Self.

Young adults today are subconsciously trained how to be 'cool' based on standards that will provide some media with personal and monetary gain. It is easy for them to accomplish this when they have learnt to identify all of the 'fun buttons', and to continuously push them. No stressful effort is required. Simultaneously, older adults meant to represent wisdom and consciousness are discretely reminded everyday that their 'natural metamorphosis' is terrible and of no good value.

When you do not own a life that is yours, it is very easy for someone else to walk in and impose another way of life onto you.

Reinventing a Self is not based on a collective opinion, survey or poll. Reinventing a Self requires the ability to sit in the company of Self. It requires trust and the ability to listen in a quiet environment to what our bodies and minds are telling us with the supervision of the consciousness. There are always ample opportunities to reinvent Self. The best place to start is by getting rid of what no longer serves us. When we trash what we have been carrying, but no longer need, we have a lot more storage space for experiences that will better serve our Self.

The cleanup is followed by a process of illuminating our innate passion, which is added to all that we will do next. Reinventing is newness. There is no room for old when we live in the mode of reinventions. However, the reinvention of Self does not alter the core. It remains steady like a true North on your compass of individuality.

Celebrating Self is an ongoing event in a reinvented world. Celebrating birthdays every year is a fun thing to do, when we are practicing our math skills.

We must seek celebrations for the bite-sized moments of wonder in life, as it unfolds its gifts to us outside of our logical plan. Celebrate your quirks, your imbalances, your mistakes, your silliness, your contradictions, your ever-changing looks and abilities, while remaining true to your grounded and firm core as a unique individual.

When I choose to live by reinventing myself continuously in the life time that is mine, I gain new experiences as well as an inclusive service to polish my older experiences.

'Old' is synonymous with good things like collected memories, as well as not so good things, such as something that once had value but no longer does. When we choose to live by repeating experiences that have no value to guide, to inspire, to lead, and to be a part of the solution, we are 'old', no matter our age. Another description of 'old' is anytime you choose to no longer learn, to no longer create, to no longer dream, and to no longer change for the better.

I will be 'old' the day I am no longer in the company of passion. Only I can decide what will no longer bring me passion.

38.
Clear Out Your Baggage. Remove Habits That Do Not Serve You

Travel light or travel heavy, you choose.

When travelling with a lot of baggage, you are limited in speed of movement. If you had to run to meet any unexpected and beautiful opportunity, you could be left behind with the impeding weight of the baggage. Worrying about the loss of your belongings could affect your mental and emotional health, as well as the overall travel experience.

Try boarding a train that is stopping for only three minutes with many heavy bags. If you have to bring everything you need and possibly own in tandem with the comfort of your normal life, why bother to travel? Why not just stay in your comfort zone? By travelling light, you are able to care for your health a little bit better, starting with less weight encumbering your shoulders, and fewer things to worry about that are in your possession. You would be able to manoeuvre easier through all kinds of circumstances, and be available for more transport options, such as riding a bullock cart or riding a yak.

The objective for travel is an important factor to consider for the different types of travellers. The light travellers can accept spontaneous opportunities to enrich their souls by interconnections with diverse people, places and ways of being, and to delight in all the newness. Of course, the heavy traveller can do so too, but there is added baggage, including the biggest one—the inability to shed the comfort in being needy.

In the course of our life journey, it is normal to pick up many habits and accepted ways of being as our baggage, except, of course, for those of us who are perfect.

The weight of unnecessary baggage only increases with our years of being physically alive. Habits become the most comforting companions we know. They become the old or the never changing, the 'been there, done that', the 'I am too old to change'. Do not deny your soul, body and mind the chance to experience the newness of anything.

There is little excitement in learning without a sense of passion. A bigger realisation that comes with the challenges in growing older is not the cool grey hair, or the artistically developing wrinkles, it is the time spent fearing the unknown and in deciding that being a new learner is a ridiculous idea.

The most significant side-effects of olderness happen when the baggage of unneeded habits and ways of being are carried with you in your life travels. It is difficult to dispose of them because they serve as your security blanket in case you are forced to face all of the things you never liked in the history of your life.

A good example of a familiar habit is stubbornness. Stubbornness has nothing to do with ageing and it has a dual personality. One of its aspects allows for us to hold onto the good we believe in by providing us the firmness to remain true to our individual Self. This is the serving side. The other side places barriers in front of your path toward progress. It holds on tight to the idea that you are right, and that you will always be right. This side of stubbornness causes all doors leading to learning new ways to better your Self to abruptly close.

When I experience older people insisting that they be heard because they are older, it is not the best way to evoke my attention.

My attention lights up like a festive Christmas tree whenever I am in the presence of a soul who is living a lifetime of great deeds without fear of an expiry date.

The aura of a silent and wise presence is a difficult virtue and magic to market to the masses. Wisdom is not a natural side-effect of being older. Youth is not an age based on consecutively increasing numbers. The idea of youth is to be open to new ideas and to be fearless in embracing them. It is not a given condition that comes with being young.

Olderness is, in fact, a disease if it includes the symptom of a limited mind with closed doors and windows. Other symptoms include looking out from the closed Self at the life of others as if one is an expert, avoiding new perspectives that one has never chosen to understand or to accept, and remaining comfortable in avoiding the work required to restructure a new wiring system in order to adopt a way of being more purposeful than the one currently owned. Narrow-mindedness and closed thinking have a continuity that constitutes a solid bad habit and leaves no room for breathable wisdom.

In choosing to *Live Older*, you are willing to listen to every discussion as if it were the very first time. You are offered an opportunity to create and to collect stories, including all the dark and not-so-nice bits; to share or to remodel in silent reflection before adding to a new conversation, filing it with the collection of memories from your mind.

Bad days are bad days, no matter your age. In times of darkness you will view yourself with possibly more criticism. Add extra light, and keep finding more ways to do so. The day will pass and a new one will come by. It is required that you make an obligation to yourself to evolve positively in a world constantly transforming.

Bad habits, on the other hand, get worse as they become older. If we choose to live life with them, they make everything more ugly about ourselves in the eyes of others, especially those closest to us. It is time to repossess or to reinvent new purposeful habits of being, while discarding habits that are stagnant and the ones that have become old in their uselessness. It is never too late to say 'good riddance' to unwanted weight.

In your newly found lightness, may your steps tread with meaning, and may your eyes shine with a powerful sense of contentment!

39.
Get High On Self-Generated Energy

The world we live in is moving fast.

We live in our physical bodies through its spinning madness, and it affects us. We talk fast. We eat fast. We walk fast. We make love fast. We enter relationships fast, and we come out of relationships fast. We earn money fast. We consume fast. We communicate fast. We can even find a friend fast. At the same time, we are sick earlier. We are quickly depleted of energy. We need artificial highs to get us going. We need to be intoxicated in order to feel anything but 'dead'. As all of this becomes a reality, we want to live 'better than ever' because of the illusion that our bodies are not made to naturally deteriorate.

You must understand how to invest in every precious drop of energy. Yes, you must learn it. Begin with an investment in time for Self. Accompany this with an understanding that energy is a result of a continuous process. We need to understand the fact that positive and vital energy is not a miracle product one can buy and consume as if it is a superpower that is beckoned when one needs it in a time of crisis.

In order to *Live Older*, live with the understanding that whether life is a continuum or not is not of our immediate concern because we are designed not to know. Instead go deeper within your Self where the soul does not age like our physical body and mind are required to do. When you are able to connect with the energy of your soul, there is no test required to confirm its existence nor its age. Here, the quantity of energy available as fuel is dependent upon each unique composition, as well as the care given in using it wisely and in knowing one's limitations.

Lacking energy is not a required symptom in growing older. The condition certainly does not creep up overnight, as if it were a birthday gift to one whose age has reached a high number. A lack of energy is a consequence of chemical malfunctions that are a result of how you manage your physical body and mind.

The sacred art of feeding myself is one of the most important areas for energy gain. The act of feeding involves not only food and drink, but also the breath of life that I take for each good time and for each bad time that I am living.

A Natural High on Energy

A Sprinkle of Ideas

1. Avoid food and drink that makes your chemistry weak.

2. You are the expert of your body's wisdom.

3. Keep away from toxic-minded people.

4. Act silly.

5. Let go of seeking perfection.

6. Find what you love to do. In time, if you do not love it anymore, be respectful of its lessons, say goodbye, and leave.

7. Spend time in silence.

8. Spend time in the company of Nature.

9. Keep the body and the mind moving: the bowels, the fluids, thoughts, ideas, knowledge, feet, muscles, senses, curiosity, love, and unexpected bursts of laughter.

10. Laugh loudly and openly. Allow your soul to partake in its pleasure.

11. Stop eating before you feel full.

12. Be aware of what you allow into your body, mind and soul.

13. Do not trick your body and mind into believing that you are in danger. This can be created when watching a horror movie, for example. The body's smart systems will naturally release backup to prepare you for your survival. Any security system, including the one within your body, is limited, and it uses a whole lot of energy. Save this energy reserve for when you truly need it.

14. Move more than you are sitting in a day.

15. Learn something new about your Self as often as possible.

16. Learn about the subtle energy systems within us, and use this knowledge to assist us in our healing.

Energy that is self-generated is a reserve not to be taken lightly. Pack it in the backpack of Living Older. Have fun and use it well. Bon voyage!

40.
Fear Less or Start Dying

Fear is the silent four-letter 'F' word.

One word not heard, but seriously felt by many; it is a necessary emotion that reminds us about what we hold dear. It draws a fixed boundary between what we know and what we do not know yet. It protects us from placing ourselves in a situation that may not serve us. Fear also has the ability to paralyse the Self, keeping it in lock down mode away from living experiences.

As I *Live Older*, I know that there are certain fears present in me since I was a child. I adopted the fears from events I did not yet understand, and it is the reason why it is shelved in the fear cupboard of my memories. It may take me a lifetime to fully understand these fears, or maybe, I do not need to understand them; either way, I may have to carry them with me always.

There is a gift my experiences in living have given to me—not all fears are equal.

When the shivering and the quivering appear, stick your tongue out at the fear that does not serve you, and embrace the fear that keeps your energy up and moving.

I can place my fears into two categories: those self-imposed by my limitations, and those I do not yet understand. I am now able to work on those self-imposed fears, a task far from easy, but I have started trying, and I will keep on trying.

Sometimes I am afraid because I am ignorant of the fear. For example, I may be afraid of snakes. Upon understanding the fear, I discover that I have insufficient knowledge about snakes. How can I be afraid of something I do not truly know? My 'school for the fear of snakes' has been limited to movies, images and limited stories one hears amongst all The Noise. Is it acceptable to be afraid of something because you have been influenced by someone else's limited ideas and analysis?

Perhaps you are afraid of death. You may spend your entire life discovering what happens after death so as to relieve your fear; however, in so doing, you may miss the important idea of death needing to remain a mystery. In pursuit of its revelation, you may forget to live the present life you are meant to live. When you live this present life to the best of your honour and ability, you may not need to be afraid of dying.

Throughout my life, I have been blessed with the opportunity to learn and to speak different languages. However, it is only recently that I have realised how vital it is to understanding each country's cultures, to notice how the difference in language (without direct translation) provides an insight into a culture that lives and embodies it. The willingness to be new in learning provides me with a fear-free status to be present at the START line for the possibility of new introductions. I find many advantages with this freedom to be new in learning when applied to understand religion and other firm beliefs.

We cannot use fear as an excuse to criticise. Fear is baggage, full of one's limitations. This is relevant to all that is self-limiting. We need to know our limitations in possessing the accurate knowledge behind each belief and principle before we are even allowed to utter a whisper of criticism.

While you *Live Older*, there will be many more events, ideas, and things to fear. It makes sense if you believe the longer you live the more there is to fear. It may also be a good time to learn to stop fearing. When given its due respect, fear is a good thing. Fear that keeps me away from what, and who, may harm me is a precious gift.

When you use fear as an excuse to create comfortable limitations for your Self, you are already precipitating the process of dying a slow death.

Breathe, relax your shoulders, erase the visual of fear from your mind, ground your feet firmly on the ground, unclench your fists, get up, retake ownership of your Self, and face the many rough edges you need to squeeze past in order to be who you need to be.

41.
Do Not Lose Your Voice Even If No One Is Listening

Acknowledgement of Self and others is an important component of living. Our presence in this world must have a purpose. The size of the purpose is irrelevant to its existence. It is a purpose that is certainly bigger than working, paying bills and eventually retiring from this worldly lifetime process. If there is no purpose, why waste beautiful feelings of passion, love, despair and the many languages of the soul?

Purpose is not a box in which every individual's uniform measure is taken. Often, we know this, we really do. We receive subtle intuitive messages hinting at our strengths and weaknesses, even if in practice we unconsciously ignore them. The palette of life's colours has a mixture of both good times and not so good times. Each of our reactions to how these colours affect us is dependent on who we are at a given moment, which will affect the unique way we will re-act or pro-act to what we are facing. It is important to note that our best and natural reactions to life circumstances are opportunities that introduce us to the purpose we may have been seeking. In order to arrive at this point, we first need to set forth, place ourselves in both easy and difficult situations, and simply live.

To *Live Older*, change and the unknown have to be constant companions. In living your experiences, you will learn to accept that instability is a natural way of being. The further you continue to push your Self toward unknown areas in living, the more you will feel closer to life than to death.

The problem, if any, is that we try to define stability as a perfect phenomenon. We move through life endeavouring to attain this illusion, with constant disappointment, first and foremost in ourselves, followed immediately by disappointment in the ones we love.

In being present with your individuality, it is important to learn and to respect silence. This state of silence, a superpower in which you must invest, will assist in creating balance as you walk the unknown roads in the continuous journey of life. This state of silence is a powerful practice in enforcing the power of your presence. This silence is not about keeping quiet and being uninterested or disconnected from your place on this planet. Instead, it is a creative space for deep contemplation that is available within you during the downtimes as you explore the constant transitions of your life journey. It is in this space of silence where you begin to hear the melodic voice of your existence. It is a sound that comes from deep within you. It can be powered by nothingness, or it can be powered by the soul through the emotions you bring into what you say.

In the marketing of many goods and services today, a voice that is rooted in nothingness, or empty of real and powerful values, can be designed for attention subtly via the psyche. This voice is easily heard by anyone who is not making much effort to seek an identified 'something', or is someone who has lost a sense of conscious purpose and connection. Because it is superficial, the message can be designed to gain such a person's immediate attention by fulfilling their desperate need. This voice can be imposing because it knows its audience. It knows that a person who is lost or disconnected is desperately seeking to fulfil the conscious emptiness within them. It can design itself to attract, entertain, and soothe these senses with false promises to fill their missing needs. When we are in a state of vulnerability without being grounded by our consciousness, it is easy to fall prey to attractive messages of the selfish and profiteering individuals.

Alternatively, it is difficult to push a person off-balance who is consciously grounded and connected. This target market usually does not appear on the list of quick scams because it would be a difficult task to entice them with Noise. The voice for this target market reaches the 'deep withins'. It has a magnetic ability towards being grounded by individual purpose.

A voice that is rooted deep within, and that is accompanied by the soul, cannot be mistaken. It will tug at you, even if you are trying hard to avoid it.

This voice does not seek an audience. It is too busy practicing a dance to a rhythm that resonates with the orchestra of the Universe. Anyone who needs to hear it will be there. This voice, when heard, inspires another being to straighten up, to be connected and to live better. It is a facilitated soul-to-soul communication.

We all have a voice. Its volume is regulated by the Self, which carries this voice. When we are insecure, our voice will match the tone of our insecurity. When we are one with awareness, our voice will represent this balance as we speak. When we are in touch with our soul, our voice echoes its vibe.

As we live the adventures offered in a life, we sometimes go astray from our intended objectives. Such is a normal state for those of us who are imperfect, as we dance with so many options, choices, struggles and emotionally turbulent rides. Self-awareness and self-centring are prerequisites in creating an art form of becoming astray. These qualities will provide us with stability in the time of our weakness so as not to adopt another, more imposing voice to take over our soul.

To adopt the voice of another and make it our own is an easy feat when we are not present in our mind and body. Being limited in the ability and/or the possibility to make ourselves heard, we give the bigger voice our stage presence. It is no wonder why the young are so attracted to making videos and posting them for others to see and hear. Upon deeper observation, you can identify that most begin to adopt a similar voice, while wanting to be better than the others within the limited perimeter of sameness. This similarity in both voice and message is gobbled up and shared by different people again and again and again. There must be millions of voices with contagious messages that need to scream in order to be heard over the noise of information we have allowed to surround us as our accepted way of being.

Finding the original voice amidst the many millions of people is a precious balm for another's soul, like knowing that there are other survivors out in a river full of piranhas.

If you have lost your voice, it is time to find it again. As you *Live Older*, you need to tune your voice to your individual soul so that you can sing its original tune for others to benefit. I am not asking you to enter a contest because your individual voice cannot be in a competition. How can you compete when we are different? How can you compete individuality within limited rules?

We could give up our original voices so as to comply with the standards of other imposing voices. We could comply with the standards of imposing voices for the fear of not being heard. Yet, for our voices to be heard, we do not need a stadium full of fans or a devoted audience. When we root our presence to where we need to be, the voice resonates. It is the sparks and the WIFI signals we emit to others. It does not need a sound. It certainly is not noisy for the ears. It attracts hungry hearts and undernourished souls to its frequency.

We look up and applaud the lives of those who put themselves up on a physical stage to sing, to dance and to act. We allow their fame to burn, while we dim our own spark with our fears and our worries about not meeting a state of perfection whose standards were created by someone else. We listen to the voice of the person as it entertains our ears. Our awareness is blinded as to whether the voice is coming from the soul of beings who, as humans, are rooted in consciousness or not. Instead, we become the unconscious kindling to their disconnected soul.

We quickly swallow our voices to hide in the shadows of judgement from others. We give the power to those who benefit from imposing their voices onto us. We lie numb as we lower the volume of our voices until only we can hear it fading from within us. We begin to hold our breath more and more tightly as we start to bury our souls into darkness far away from the rays of life. Our inner voice knows when to be silent.

It knows when to be quiet even when the will to be loud is strong.

Live Older and in all politeness stick your tongue out at fear that does not serve you. Kiss the fear that keeps your energy up and moving. Close your ears to what is deafening. Find silence, your very own silence. The voice you have is yours. It is not a property of another unless, of course, you give it to them. Your voice speaks for Self. It markets you. It protects you. It represents you. If you are full of &*^%, your voice is full of &*^%. If you are full of happiness, your voice is full of happiness. If you are negative, your voice is negative. If you are positive, your voice is positive. Pay good attention to the lyrics of a song. The words that make up a song complement strongly the nature of the person singing it.

We need to hear more voices attuned to their own individuality, the ones that have the powerful ability to create an effect of beauty and positive change in another. We need voices that resonate in pride and respect of Self and all living beings. We also need voices that have no need to convert others to be like them, but instead, seek to inspire others to become their own unique voices.

All it takes is one person listening to this amazing voice, starting with you, the owner of your very own voice.

The Existence of Your Voice

Put Up A Show

1. Do not give your power in ownership of Self to people who put your voice down.

2. In order to be your voice, listen very carefully to everything around you, and feel.

3. Sing to your Self. There is no need to aim for perfection, nor to be someone else.

4. Sing loudly to your Self. Feel your soul.

5. Sing louder to your Self. Feel your Self connect with your soul.

6. Practice conscious breathing.

7. Walk with your eyes looking straight ahead rather than looking downward.

8. Keep your shoulders back and rib cage feeling open at the chest.

9 Read out loud to children or to your pets.

10. In a day, include moments of silence and reflection in order to connect with your inner voice, your purpose, and your passions.

11. Discover ways your voice can work for the good of other living beings.

12. Love your Self for all of its smooth and rough edges.

My Voice

I am here

In my recognition of Self.
In the body that has been given to me
from a source I may yet have to explore
or perhaps never.
In the mind that opens up windows and
doors for me
to have sensual feasts.
I speak
Words that represent my insides to the
outsides.
Forgive me, if my words are limited.
It may be that I have not understood yet
what my voice can do.
At present,
I may use my voice to escape
a pain that sits deep inside my heart.
It beats chords of despair,
of defence against my Self
or against another.
Compliment me not,
if my words seem to flow
like life-saving water from an oasis
in the midst of parched deserts.
Not yet, at least.
Until I know
how not to let it all get to my head.
What matters is that

I am here.
See me.
Hear me.
My soul may be trapped
in a body or a mind
that does not look attractive to you.
I assure you that
I am here.
My soul is present.
Deep
inside the crumbling of my body and my
mind.
I am here.

Know that I am.

42.
Stop Lying To Your Self

A lie is a very useful tool.

For children and naïve people, the ability to lie comes to good use when they want to do certain things that they are not allowed to do, but they really want to do so very much. A lie allows us to almost have it all. The childhood phase passes very quickly. Its naïve innocence is replaced with the awareness of how lying causes pain to others, accompanied by a horrible sense of guilt.

To *Live Older*, be firm in laying out standards concerning the interpretation of your unique presence.

Begin to comprehend that the journey of life offers you ample opportunity to learn, to make mistakes, to shine and to look stupid.

There is nothing wrong with looking stupid, especially if the cause of the stupidity provided you with the courage to go where you have never been before.

By exploring these paths through a fog of uncertainty and confusion, you will begin to identify some useful tools that will assist you in this journey. A lie is an easily accessible tool. However, before you choose to pick it up as a tool, check in with your awareness. A lie will provide you with instant gratification. In a competitive game of who is winning and who is losing, a lie carries with it a very important and high standing. A lie is a great ally for superficial perfection.

In a story or a movie, a good scenario that grips our hearts and emotions will often include lies and deceit in the script. This serves a purpose to tug at our emotions while the script continues to lead us towards an eventual path of good and all that is beautiful.

To *Live Older*, stop taking the shortcuts. Stop searching for the quick fix. Be with the pain of life experience. Start practicing a life of free falling. Accept that life is not the destination but a part of an on-going journey. Begin to see the unimportance of lies. The only place a lie is taking you is to one far away from your Self; far away from your ugliness, your weaknesses, your mistakes, and all of the aspects that are vital to a life of beautiful imperfections, which you must embody in order to live with your soul.

Staying true to your Self requires immense courage: to clean up the mess of the mistakes you make, to be laughed at when you choose not to follow where your soul does not direct you, and to face the obstructions in your path from the various disasters that you will encounter in living your life. When you choose to stop lying, it is your Self you begin to pick up from the ground. As you dust off your knees, you can now see clearly and perhaps avoid the next fall.

Even if this transition takes a longer time, the lessons you learn from this opportunity become an additional gift. It is a gift you receive only by pushing your abilities further than is comfortable in order to be the best you can be. Non-stop!

The only person you face in aloneness is your Self.

One of the greatest highs in living is when you look in the mirror and you see your beautiful soul shine from within with all of your worldly imperfections.

An affirmation that life is a magical experience indeed.

43.
Live A Life Of The Magical Unknown

In a world of quick, accessible information, there are no limits; there is no mystery and no suspense, at least it seems this way. I do not believe that curiosity and access to readily available information are 'best friends forever'. In order to be curious, I have to bring out all of my senses to play with the mind and even with the body. The most fun I have had in being curious is at times when I do not really know where I am going next. The times when I had to experience the answer rather than to find it theoretically while sitting in the midst of someone else's limited research. I do not mean that I was lost or confused. I am talking about times I choose to be outside of what is my comfort zone, and way outside of my expertise.

We seem to be zapping the vast ocean of endless online information to appease our senses, which are becoming more and more numb. Our senses are evolving to become so numb that watching living beings be brutally killed is a part of our entertainment in the movies we watch, in the games we play and in the news we read. Acquisition of useless knowledge is a favourite choice in determining our human values. Too much of it or too little of it equals to something of meaning to all of us in our daily life operations.

We surround ourselves with many friends, most of whom have a tendency to disappear when life looks a little like a painting that is coloured outside of the lines.

Meanwhile, we live life with no conscious navigation system, and by operating on autopilot we give up Self to our devices for pleasure, information and a life mate, if required. What do we do with the unknown? Mostly, we can pretend not to think about it by making our minds overly busy. If for some reason life sends a predicament our way, the first and the easiest thing to do is to fear it, which is followed by doubt that is created by the many conflicting expertise of others. Our unique minds continue to 'fish' for knowledge and answers in an infinite ocean of information with a limited amount of fish in the form of appropriate ideas or a functional theory amongst many floating useless ideas and theories.

To *Live Older*, begin to accept life for all of its differing colours. Learn to attain skills through living experiences in the unknown or in areas outside of your comfort zone. Live with an awareness of the moment you are living in. Learn to consciously put the voices of your past, and the fears of your future, in line with where you are right now. Bring them all together in the tempo of the present where your vision, senses, and choices can come together to affect the life you are choosing to live.

There is no need to pretend that you are not afraid when you arrive at a place of the unknown; instead, become 'switched on' and grounded in taking the immediate action that is led by your consciousness. Seek quiet away from worldly din, and connect to the power of your source as you recharge yourself with the new energy you need to create the new story of your life adventure.

Calm the thoughts regarding tomorrow by grounding them in the truth of today's preparations.

The biggest unknown of all unknowns is death. Due to the lack of sufficient healthy and intelligent conversations concerning death, there is a gaping hole left in the completion of the circle of life. In *Living Older*, when the finale of your life comes into question, you will have the experience required to be calm and to trust that you lived every day alight with passion, meaning and kindness.

I do not know, and I do not believe any other human being really knows what happens to us when we physically die; I am not interested in knowing. I am more interested to live my life in the best way I can. With this in mind, my imagination becomes more creative. I laugh more. Fear abandons my being, leaving me totally available for what I need to do right now

44.
Adversity &
La Belle Vie.
Who Is Good
& Who Is Bad?

Any beloved story comprises both good times and bad times.

The combination provides a complete story that holds our attention. A living life must include some of both the good and the bad, with extra options for the confused.

Who determines what is good and what is bad for your life? If you believe material wealth to be an important accumulation to have in the journey of life, it would make sense to judge your Self to be 'lowly' for not having enough, or any of it. You will lack the ability to see that by having less of it, you could have more time to experience many other aspects of a rich life well lived.

If you believe that having children is important in completing the purpose of who you are, it is tempting to judge your Self to be 'purposeless' should you be unable to have children. You will lack understanding of your bigger purpose, perhaps one that involves many orphaned and abandoned children who need your love and attention, or your purpose may be spending more time looking after the neglected planet.

When life offers a slice of what does not taste so good on the tongue immediately, we can either spit it out and throw a tantrum about how life is bad or we can continue to chew on it and perhaps discover seconds later that what initially tasted bad is followed by an amazing feeling you would never have discovered had you not been in trust of life's offerings for you.

If we believe that bad things happen only to bad people, we must truly believe that we are bad when bad things happen to us. Such a belief provides us with a great opportunity to punish ourselves with self-hatred, and a good reason to bury ourselves in excuses that could limit us further.

In *Living Older*, you would seek to be consciously aware of what each experience brings along for us. You need to learn that an answer, or clarity, is not always obvious, and certainly not always immediate. Herein lie opportunities to strengthen your trust, as well as time to practice patience and in so doing, you may be provided special vision to see the unique strength an experience gifts you.

There are many stories of adversity. Our perception of these adversities is often a switch that is in our self-control. The description of each adversity in itself is a unique one. The visual lens between not having any water to drink at all versus the inability to find water with sparkles in it is wide or narrow depending on the power of the lens you are looking through.

The French expression 'la belle vie' can mean surrounding oneself with immense material pleasure. It can also mean to be alive out in the Universe amongst friends, both new and old; and family, both new and old; all gathered around a big table sharing crafted food and conversations. Here, presence and connection are invited, while no measurements or comparisons are required. The latter is my personal interpretation.

You need only to choose perseverance and determination to stay true to a unique journey of Self, and a feeling of utmost contentment will be your companion.

The Emotional

Laugh
out so loud
as dark clouds pass.
Tears
melt my heart
as I live with what hurts.
I love so big
because you guide
the orchestra of my heart.
My strength grows big
because you sing melodies
that make my mind flutter.
A woman I am in abundance.
A man I need
who will plant your seed
and
proudly watch you flourish
giant walls
and big leaded hearts.
Making love
get up
again
and
again.

45.
Spoil
Yourself
With Self
Love

I have had to provide love for myself from a very young age, way before I understood the philosophical notion of loving a Self.

I have respected Self and accepted my individuality early in life. At this time, I had no idea that the priceless value in giving of my love to others who have come to share it with me would increase enormously as a result of loving my Self.

The belief made sense for a long time until it was time to graduate to bigger lessons in life. When my beautiful second marriage ended, I knew in my mind and my soul that it was the right thing to do. My heart took many more years to come to terms with it, while my body began a slow process in healing from the symptoms of dis-ease that came along on the ride of a relationship that was no longer meant to be. The reactions of my emotions were the ones I least expected. The years following the breakup provided for me many dimensions in lessons of how far emotions could stretch themselves. There is a lot of pain in losing a beautiful relationship with a history of many years.

In times of trouble, there is a tendency to not let go of anything that provides us with safety, comfort and consistency.

In a short time, I felt I was ready to move on to another relationship. Love is what I needed, and I had so much to offer. Why wait? Life is short, right? Yes, life is short. Life lessons, on the other hand, are many. Some of them last a long time.

With the passing of some more time, I came to understand what I needed was not an **ambulance relationship**. I did need a lot of love, and lots and lots of care. I needed care for my invisible deep wounds and for my bleeding heart. In order to survive the pain, I needed to complain about how unfair life had been to me. I needed lots and lots of extra attention as the ground beneath me was crumbling.

Like many of us, in my time of weakness, I believed that the natural place from which to get some healing would be in another relationship. Is this not the meaning of a relationship? To give and to take, while often blurring the lines as to who is giving more and who may be receiving less. Having been a partner in a good and beautiful relationship, I had outsourced all of the love I needed to someone else. Is this not the meaning of trust and commitment? When the relationship ended, it made sense that my love support system was failing and turning me 'blue' from the suffocation of not being 'loved' by someone. It makes so much sense that predators seeking to take advantage of vulnerable people come looking for those who find themselves in this situation.

I rode the ups and the downs of the aftermath of my beautiful relationship as it took me to very dark places through which I began to see the shining light, and the more I looked towards this light, my dormant Self-love was rudely awakened. It was confused when it awoke from its deep slumber, having lost all of its ability to rationalise the outcome of what had just happened. In a quiet panic, it tried desperately to search for another place where it could lie dormant. It took a year and a half before I truly began to understand the vital lesson from this experience, from this tornado of emotional confusion.

Very, very slowly in the silence of my sorrow, I began to relearn the lessons of love. I began to see that I was the only one who could give myself what I needed to feel good. I began to enjoy the company of my breath again. I dropped the essence of desperation that was sprinkled on my emotions without the knowledge of my mind. I began to learn new lessons in standing balanced on the soles of my feet. I began to observe things around me differently. Mostly, I was strengthening my heart strings while we experienced new lessons together as one.

I began to feel richer with my senses. Passion is a fire that needs to burn, and I was getting to know the passion that was kindled by just being me. It is not a fire exclusive to a romantic relationship, as we are often made to believe. Loving someone else is not the only place to burn this fuelling passion. Doing something for your Self, for Nature, or for someone else is a fulfilling place to share the energy of this wonderful experience.

I began to fall in love with my Self.

It is the kind of love that keeps me stable, a love that teaches me that in order to extend my hand out to someone else to share, I need to first be of great value to my Self. It has taught me that my life support system is my responsibility. There is good reason we are asked to first place the oxygen masks on ourselves before helping another. It keeps me assured that no matter what happens next, I have nothing to fear from my own company, and that I am never alone in the company of my conscious Self.

Loving my Self assures me that I am not afraid to love. I know that my love will be present in abundance for another because first I learned to love my beautifully imperfect Self. It leaves me confident, and not desperate to attract whoever enters the dance of love with me.

There is deep power in knowing that you are present for your Self.

Spoil Your Self

A Sprinkle of Suggestions

1. Keep in mind that loving Self is not a love that stems from Self-obsession.

2. Look into the mirror and tell your Self, "I love you (your name)."

3. Treat your Self to beauty, but do not get overwhelmed with its cathartic addiction.

4. Seek courage in the company of Nature.

5. Seek support from Nature.

6. Find your Self a purposeful way to give to Nature, or to another being outside of your Self.

7. Do everything you want to do in the company of your Self.

8. Immerse your healing energy towards Self-care.

9. Be very kind to your Self.

10. Be polite with your Self.

11. Celebrate the freedom to fart, burp or other such bodily excretions in a space that is truly yours.

12. Be privileged to be in the company of you.

13. If really necessary, direct a movie where you are the star (Refer to #1 before proceeding). No one can stop you but your Self!

46.
Be
Fearlessly
In Love

Love is a small four-letter word that can cause war, destruction, goodness, and incredible beauty.

It has the power to make a big difference, but also to destroy. Commercially, it generates a lot of money with special occasions like Valentine's Day and weddings. Oh, what we do for it, and who we become without it! The lessons in love seem never-ending. We have a tendency to believe that love is a destination. Whether a boyfriend/girlfriend, marriage or a life partner, each represents a destination for being in love.

As the years of life progress, we begin to experience that as simple a word as 'love' is, it can be mighty complicated. We create concepts from the word to confirm that now we are finally happy, that we are no longer terribly alone. When it does not meet our interpretations, we begin to feel cheated, as if hope was nothing but a mirage. We then shift the gears of our emotions, reversing them into sad and angry ones. We may continue to take in the burst of energy and use it to build high, heavily guarded walls around our Self so as never to be in the company of love again.

In my own story, I picked myself up and believed the solution lay in seeking the next relationship; the alternative of which was to give up on love completely. I knew immediately that giving up on love was not a decision I would make.

When you love life, love is one of its magical components.

In making the choice to look for a new relationship, where I could give of myself completely, I was expecting to receive a love I wanted to fit my required template in return. In due time, I learned that this was a self-destructive strategy. There was no benefit for me to be in a fast-food type love that was easy to acquire if I remained unconscious and in denial concerning my deeper needs. I had been intent on learning more about love's many shape-shifting forms. This is like impatiently waiting to replace the original parts in a car that is no longer in production; a very difficult feat to accomplish, costly, time consuming, and yet, the alternative in choosing cheap fake parts for the car would not allow it to go too far. The gift in learning to love my Self came from this long self-doubting search.

If you have not had the opportunity to love your Self, start now. It is not the easiest act to accomplish but in its perseverance there are an abundance of priceless gifts.

When you love your Self, you are able to take some of this good, glowing love to share it with someone else who needed just your brand of love and together you will create a great fusion of sensual pleasures. Loving someone for the beauty of shared love is a process of giving and receiving, without scales or measurements. This is not the love that serves as a crutch to your sensitive ego, or the love that is present because of neediness; nor is it a love that keeps you on a treadmill of worry, or the love that keeps you safe from your fear of being alone. When you love your Self, there is no worry about being loved in return.

Loving your Self allows you to *Live Older*.

You can feel lost and unloved even in a serious relationship. This type of relationship is even harder for your Soul than to be alone with Self.

We fall into love and we make commitments. If we are to live in the present moment, and if we consider our life a journey in which we have no map or directions, how do we guarantee our commitments until 'death do us part'? As years pass, we evolve and the circumstances around us evolve. We get hurt. We get bored. As individuals, in a relationship, one may choose to live many more stories, while the other's story may be about always remaining the same person.

If you remain in love throughout the different phases that time tests you, the only thing to affirm is that you continue to do the best you can do everyday and every moment, of your relationship. However, if there is a question, a doubt, a wonder, or a sense of claustrophobia, it does not mean that you have failed. Instead, the intuitive gift of awareness is communicating with you to shine a little extra light and to 'check in' to the source of your feelings.

We grow, evolve and make choices that best suit us as an individual first, then as a couple and as a family. *Live Older* in reflecting on the changing images and roles of who you become. Add to it an awareness that witnesses the many rushes of emotions and levels of breathing on the roller coaster ride of love.

In a relationship with another, we notice changes as intricate as little nuances. We begin to notice the changes in our partner before they have come to terms with them within their Self.

Here are some important questions to ponder: Are the individuals involved in the relationship creating beauty? Are you maintaining the relationship to keep the peace, while your mind and body are at war within your Self? Are you afraid of being labelled as a failure, or as someone who rocked the boat? The answers we provide are personal and individual to ourselves.

Whatever the answer, courage is required. For those of us with children, specific doubts start to surface: 'The kids will suffer'. For those of us with financial woes, we are fearful of the loss of assets and a certain comfortable lifestyle. There are also the fears of the loss of friends, of misery and in particular, of being alone for the rest of our lives.

The truth is that a dead relationship is a dead one.

It requires 'dead people' to keep a dead relationship in operation. Everything about it is fake and staged. Would you be good examples of love and relationships for your kids by remaining in such a relationship? What is your personal definition of suffering? Is it a lifetime worth of servitude to dread, or is it a short-lived pain due to the removal of a relationship that has become a 'toxic growth' in the journey of your life?

Only in the company of awareness are you able to realise that you, or the other individual in the relationship is no longer a source of enlightenment in the partnership. Instead, this lack of enlightenment has come to feel like a piece of heavy luggage in the journey of a life. Awareness will also bring with it wisdom, which will guide you to the time to say 'adieu,' with respect and love for what was sublime, as you move on to separate journeys. Each individual will mourn on a deeper level a beautiful end to the shared chapters of life, while moving forward individually toward the hope of another new day in being better living beings.

Why do we not celebrate the divorce of an ended partnership like we do a wedding? A heart that is broken now will journey a long way through many lessons toward a more complete Self tomorrow. There is no excuse for turning ourselves into miserable beings in the name of love and commitment. Respect, integrity and responsibility will be easier to provide for each other when we understand that life is larger than the man-made box of social rules.

To *Live Older*, be the sole designer of how you live in partnership with those you invite to join the relationship paths of your life journey. When in transition from a broken love, experience the habit of pampering your Self as the only remedy available to assure your wild soul that you are important. Only the Self knows to be quiet as you affirm the damages and the blessings this broken love brought to you. The practice of loving your Self is the best confidence building exercise to prepare you for the next phase in love with another.

Loving Self is not a love from need, but a love offered as a gift. Vulnerability is expansive when we are in need of love; we are willing to take part in actions, or to be with people we otherwise would not be with. When fearful, as long as someone tells us they love us, we believe them, even if deep down our heart's essence is trying to tell us to be aware; that we may be travelling on ground we do not really want to stay on during our larger life's journey.

We restart at the point of Self-love again and again, anytime and all the time. Love and Self are two common words uncommonly found together in the messages around us. In *Living Older*, you are never afraid of loving and of giving and sharing of your Self. You learn to become calm in inviting it to come your way.

Love is an important emotion that needs to be cultivated every moment of our living lives. It augments the senses when shared with another person in the journey we call the beautiful life. We learn to offer it to someone else other than to Self. If, in the beginning, it is offered from a place of calm and an inner stability, there is always a probability that the foundation upon which it is built will shake from some quakes that take place, as is the nature of all that is love, in the journey of a lifetime.

Develop the habit of loving Self. Take the courage to receive love for yourself from Self instead of waiting in regret for someone to come offer it to you. Discard the illusion that interprets love for Self is only available from someone else.

Know who you are as a unique soul outside of a relationship with another. Be willing to create the design of your life the way you want it. Accord your Self some quality time with your attention. Be alone but not lonely. Be alone but not in need. Enjoy your own company and be in love with the design of Self. These are practices that will bring varying lessons during an entire lifetime like a continuing piece of art.

When the opportunity arises to share our beautiful selves with another, we are not afraid to present ourselves in the glory of our celebration of Self, which is the best gift of love. To love is beautiful. It is a confirmation that all the complexities of being human are worthy of acceptance and celebration first by the Self, and then by another. To love fearlessly is a powerful gift offered to another.

Start with an awareness of who you are. You have the ability to own the individual life, however it is designed, and to accept being alone as a required process in the journey of living a life, rather than supposing it to be a punishment. When you learn to love your Self, you are aware of a standard required for your life. It becomes easier to keep up the standard. A fearless love is a true alchemy that you have to offer to the Universe. A loved Self that is shared with another loved Self is truly magical.

Loving in the absence of fear is incredibly uplifting and nourishing for our souls.

Such love offers, to every human being who decides to take it up, a possibility to share our holistic selves, our lives, our dreams, our interests, our individualities, our pain, our troubles, our strengths and our weaknesses, earnestly with another.

There is no discrimination, nor are there limits for this love to take place. When you first discover love, you want lots of it. When you get slapped and hit by love, you begin to enforce the many ways to fear it. There is nothing more rejuvenating and self-evolving than the experience of love at any point in the journey of a life.

So why do we stop falling in love? If you are ready to share your journey in life, *Live Older* with a partner of choice; someone who is not carrying baggage full of a regretted past, or someone with no purpose, no new thoughts, or no excitement towards the idea of renewal. If your present relationship does not show the promise of *Living Older* together, it is time to create a new story. If you are happy with a life partner, now may be a good time to create new vows about *Living Older* together. The human heart 'glows' when it is fulfilled, comforted, calmed and nurtured by another beautiful heart. Love freely. Love fearlessly. If you feel it, explore it while remaining firm on the foundations of your love for Self.

The knight in shining armour had it all wrong. His armour embedded his heart so deeply that he did not know how to love. He could not feel the pain and the joy of his heart throbbing every time he rescued someone else.

There is no right or wrong way to love. Love is a recipe that turns out better every time you try it.

Love Self Fearlessly

A Sprinkle of Good Ideas

1. Be proudly weird if this means that you are true to your Self.

2. Discover Self. You may find out that you do not like your job or where you live. Get excited about taking action for change.

3. If you are vulnerable, keep your mind switched on while your heart may be healing. Be aware of ill-intentioned people whose life purpose is to prey on love. Surround yourself with people who will protect your space as you heal.

4. Whatever you believe another can do for you in love, try to do it for your Self first.

5. Take your Self out.

6. Enjoy your company. If you cannot enjoy your own company how will someone else?

7. Put your abundant love towards the planet. It needs our love and our energetic assistance.

8. Find your superpower. Take the time to become incredible.

9. Liberate your Self from 'nonsensical' fears.

10. Liberate your Self from the gender roles in fairy tales and other such bedtime stories.

11. Get on a natural high with the soul.

12. Travel and meet a larger diversity of people to connect with as fellow human beings.

13. Know that love of Self requires your sole commitment.

14. Breathe an awareness of your Self.

15. Let the Universe know that you are in love with, in gratitude for, and in celebration of your life.

When the time is right, the recipient of your love is in for an awesome and magical treat!

Loving Another Fearlessly

A Sprinkle of Good Ideas

1. Experience loving your Self first.

2. If you are walking into a partnership of differences, know the strengths and the possibilities in merging the differences to become one large team of abilities.

3. Renew yourself with awareness. Renew the vision of your love constantly.

4. Love because it tingles your senses to be with a person, not because of the number of years of commitment.

5. Respect a long-term commitment. It has large value. But its name changes when love is no longer present within it. Numbers do not count here, either.

6. Create a new rule for cohabitation: two individual spaces linked to one shared space.

7. Never take any moment of beauty for granted.

8. Create an abundance of definitions for beauty.

47.
I Once Was

The words 'I once was' placed at the start of a sentence may have several meanings.

The meaning I would avoid in *Living Older* is the one that carries with it the glory of the past with no room for glory in the present. Compare each year of your life to each page in a book. Imagine a life book of 96 pages. If the "I once was" covered up to 75 percent of these pages, the remaining pages will, by design, remain empty. A reader will likely feel short-changed with the empty pages in this life book and will lose interest in the story.

Live to complete each page of the life you are given. You do not always have to go out on an extraordinary adventure in order to have an exciting story. Each day lived in full consciousness by the owner of the life is rich in story and inspiration by itself. If you adopt the feeling that you are no longer of service to anyone after your child is ready to take leave for their individual journey in life, you may be cutting short your life story. If you believe that retirement is the end of a major life purpose, you may be cutting short the story of your life.

Our world is designed around giving accolades and awards for many superficial reasons. We look for recognition in the safety of what worked in our lives, redacting the 'ugly stories' while recounting only what sounds good to our own ears, as well as to those of others. In choosing to live with "I once was", you may be hiding from the fear of the turbulence of living a good and complete life. In so doing, you may decide that there are no more stories to create. You may be limited to recycled stories of what once was.

The choice made to live consciously at each different and evolving phase in your life is like arriving at a new destination full of new possibilities to explore. Leave fear behind and bring curiosity along instead.

Know that you are able to learn something new at any time in your life. In the company of learning, you create many new stories.

If you are weak, acknowledge that weakness is a part of cultivating strength. We all live through periods of extreme weaknesses during different parts of our entire lifetime. Strength does not only reside in the physical realm where the perfect people live in the two-dimensional world of the poster, or the picture, or the selfie.

Strength is an outcome of the nourishment of the soul, an art form that never ends; instead, it only gets better and better. Continue to explore the healthy excitement and imagination that is required to feed the soul with the best possible experiences in living your life.

48. Create A Piece Of Art With No Rules Attached

Creativity is not 'schooled'. We could always try to 'school' it, but its vital energy will be missing, and it becomes something else. When we are not in touch with our own sense of creativity, we can look to attain the boxed up creativity of someone else. True creativity does not thrive within pre-determined boundaries. A product of creativity can be purchased, but creativity, in itself, cannot be bought.

The use of our Self as a canvas for expression is the original form of creativity. Express yourself with beautiful, radiant skin and sparkling eyes as a result of what you choose to eat. Be very restrictive about what goes into your body and onto it. You can also use your hair as a canvas for expression with natural dyes, your face and body with makeup and oils from the gifts of Mother Nature, as well as a creative choice for clothes that add towards the expression of your character. While keeping within societal measures of decency, there is a limitless scope for expression on the canvas of Self. *Living Older* provides the perfect time to go forth and express your Self artistically.

Leave a mark of approval. Dress up your Self with an expression that is created in an association with your soul. You are also able to create and express your Self on canvases that are outside the your physical form by choosing to create with the partnership of your hands, your mind, your emotions and your soul. Create a piece of art in harmony with your wild soul and own the original energy it exudes. Creative art is not meant for criticism based on another's expertise. Creative art is a celebration of Self. Often, we mistakenly believe that art and creativity are for others—a form of much needed income. But the accumulation of money cannot be raw creativity's first intention.

The creativity in Self knows no dividing line between what is perfect and what is not perfect. It is only when we create what is truly our original masterpiece that others who share the same or similar vibe come hovering over it in attraction and in recognition of its existence. The energy that raw creativity provides is healing. It brings out smiles. It connects us to a deeper understanding away from logic. In deciding to *Live Older*, you are free to play with creativity. Sprinkling the energy of creativity on everything you do allows for great vibes to connect you to the essence of being alive.

The Self as a Canvas

A Sprinkle of Crazy and Necessary Ideas

Hair

Colour. No Colour. Grey. Silver. Bald. Short. Long.

Keep in mind the most important aspect of expression is good health.

If hair texture is weak and sparse, keeping it long and styled although it is damaged and weak, may be linked to an unconscious 'holding on to' of the past. Shaving the head bald and painting the scalp with natural dyes allows for varied expression.

Be in the company of consciousness and remember each changing season brings with it a unique gift to experience.

Wrinkles

Wow! What natural designs. Like a thumb-print, no two are identical.

Express them with pride as they tell stories of a life you have lived thus far.

Add to these features, a smiling disposition and sparkly, curious eyes.

Eyes

Paint to add drama or to lighten nuances depending on the mood of the day.

Keep them shining as a result of care in what you feed your Self.

Clothes

Design your clothing style based on movement and expression of Self, whether they are conservative or wild is up to your chosen expression of the day

Design clothes as an expression of the soul, and to provide comfort for the physical body.

Creations

Prepare food and beverage in ways out of the ordinary.

Give your hands their much-needed value by using them to create something. Be creative with the problems you see everyday.

Sing because you have a voice. Sing for your non-critical Self.

There is no space for stagnant old when you create.

49.
Why So
Serious?

When I was little, I remember people older than me often asserting this fact by saying, 'I am older than you!'

I am not sure what the older people of that time were trying to express by repeatedly using this statement. What I do know; however, is this expression induced my personal feelings of defensiveness towards my younger age as being inadequate for the situation at hand. The other observation I remember is, if I closed my eyes to visualise an older person, the image was of someone severe and non-ticklish—the image of someone who is not allowed to laugh. In regards to my personal context, these observations are perhaps a unique legacy of having been in a boarding school.

Bringing these thoughts to the present time, I observe that one of the unnecessary adopted attributes of getting older is the 'serious look'. I do not accept that looking serious is a look that comes naturally with getting older. It seems to be more of a look that cements in permanence from a life lived thus far in seriousness; an attitude that has gotten more set in stone with age. This may explain why one does not need compulsion to adopt a serious looking face upon growing older. The serious face comes easily with an authoritative role. In many societies it is what commands respect.

I agree that respect is necessary for a life well lived, but it makes for an incomplete life just because one is older. Hence, the difference between the words older and elder: older in years, but elder in wisdom and a knowledgeable way of being.

Either way, adding a dose of good laughter feels like the entire body, mind and soul blended to provide the most nutritive and energetic shake ever! Laughter gets the soul dancing. Being serious has value in context; however, an incessant continuation of seriousness becomes tiresome for other people in its company.

The ability to lighten up gives you permission to make mistakes, and to learn from them. It provides you with the permission to be silly. Being silly gives you freedom from the heavy judgements of Self. Being an audience to the courageous, silly display of another does not carry an equal value in enhancing these superpowers for your Self. You have to take on the leading roles. When you are able to access silliness, you enhance superpowers that allow for the ability to relax and to let go of whatever does not serve you right there and then.

Laughter allows for imperfections to take centre stage so laugh lots as you choose to live more.

In learning to lighten up, you will master the art of lifting your Self through the challenges that you must face in life's journey. *Living Older* requires that you get high on living a good and full life of consciousness; a life that will be full of tears of joy, loud laughs, and ripples of good vibes, as you dance to the end of this physical journey and beyond.

How To Be Non-Serious

A Brave Suggestion

Play. Everyday.

Encourage the building of adult playgrounds with swings and slides.

Watch funny movies.

Place your Self in situations of surprise.

Watch movies that do not make sense to you. Make good fun of them.

Do things that are legally correct but considered age inappropriate, like laughing really loud, or dancing in the street.

Hum and Sing. Create and film a video of yourself, if you are inclined. Let your cells and soul vibrate to the sound of your voice.

Play tag with the people around you. Examples: at home with your children, at work with your colleagues or before a serious meeting, at the supermarket with other patrons, and keep on thinking of other ways.

Be stupid. Immerse your Self in areas where you are not an expert in knowledge or in experience.

50.
Be Anger Or
Be Happiness

Anger and joy do not have a predetermined beginning or ending. Imagine that you are carrying a backpack that is just comfortable for you on your back. As you move along in the journey of your life, begin to add all kinds of intangibles such as experiences and emotions like anger, happiness and sadness, feelings of pain, hurt and confusion. Each of these intangibles has a weight that can be felt while carrying your backpack. Continue to believe that what is positive for you is lighter in weight and what is negative for you is heavier in weight. At some point in time, this backpack you are carrying for your entire life will equal a weight of your choices in living. It would make good sense to discard the heavy weight that is not serving you. It is to your advantage to travel with the lightness of your soul as you continue your life stories. To *Live Older*, choose to live consciously and in awareness.

Life happens as it must.

You can react to life events as they happen with the limited armour in your possession or you can practice adding a moment of conscious awareness, allowing you time to pick a better strategy that adds to a contented life, rather than deducting from it.

If you practice this way of living, you will have to take full responsibility for your own actions. When you are aware of your actions, you become less afraid to live the life that is offered to you. You need not waste time hiding in a dark corner waiting for the parts you like to appear while you tirelessly hide the parts that you do not like. When you make a wrong turn, or if you are pushed to the gravel floor as a consequence of a choice you made, get up, dust off your knees and your ego. Accept this experience as one small lesson among the many in your lifetime. You do not take fear from this experience. You continue towards more experiences that bring a smile to your face without much effort. You look for the opportunity to seek this experience in multiplicity by placing the Self in unknown situations.

If you want to live the adventure of life, get rid of the heavy, bottomless burden of anger.

The Physical

Body is changing.
It has held up.
It has kept shiny.
It has made a few heads turn.

Now,
body is testing me.
It wants to know.
what I will do,
as it paints the colour of my hair with grey
reminding me to live life better
for here is not where I will stay.

Body needs to know
how I will touch
the softness of my belly.

Body works with mind.
Accomplices.
Checking to see
what I will do.

Now,
body needs me
to stand by the scars
it tattooed on me
when I gave birth
to humans
with love and with care.

Breasts that fed
and comforted,
no longer need
to hold guard.

They rest
and come at ease.

Body wants to know
the value of
its service
to me.

It has
been me.
The person
I need to be.

Chapters of my life,
now open
for
Free
Falling.

Spirit
will now take over.

Spirit
will embrace body and mind
Gently.

Together
they will ride
a life of love, of touch
and of gratitude.

Mind and Body,

Thank you for holding
My wild soul.

51.
Every Great Life Wears A Silver-ish Head!

To be unique is an attractive notion, especially for anyone beyond adolescence.

Deep inside of us, if we are listening in silence, we experience the authenticity of our soul's blueprint as we interact and connect in varying situations with different people. On the noisy superficial level; however, it is difficult to keep our uniqueness pure from adulteration. In our real world, it is the contradictions we face daily that keep us 'in check' with life. Unless we decide to leave all of this behind to live on a very high mountain secluded from all of mankind, there is a healthy circulation of choices we deal with forcing us to develop skills in perseverance, ownership, respect, humility and above all, confidence in Self. Change and learning how to deal with change, are both universal side effects that come with being human.

Some humans believe they can decide standards, create rules, and spread beliefs for all the rest of human kind.

Humans who are 'lost' of purpose are easy to herd in by people who wish to take advantage of their instability and lack of consciousness for Self. The plight of our 'lost-ness' becomes an opportunity for quick monetary gain. They feed on the senses of all who are confused about their life purpose and distracted by The Noise and numbness in their disturbed consciousness. It is usually in the physical aspect of our Self where the criticisms and the manipulative standards land. In order to achieve such personal gain, there is never time to invest in having conversations with each individual soul; that would be too difficult and time-consuming when profit margins are the objective.

In *Living Older*, reprise your individual journey with inner reflection in order to reverse daily thoughts and ideas that keep you enslaved in a system of gain for another, but not for Self.

One of the most distinguishing changes of our life cycle is the greying of hair. Yes, grey hair is a sign of an increasing age. (We are excluding premature greyness of hair due to other reasons in this context). Let us apply a logical mathematical type of questioning and reasoning here: If grey hair signifies 'increasing age', disguising grey hair must be equal to disguising 'the increasing of age'? The problem to decipher; therefore, is why would one want to disguise 'the increasing of age'?

For many years, perhaps centuries, the greying of hair has been regarded as an aesthetic eyesore. In a commercial context, the word 'age' is commonly paired with the prefix 'anti', a word that brings along with it feelings of being deeply unwanted and hated. What a ridiculous idea! It is like saying that we do not want the beauty of autumn's changing colours, so let's get some paint and colour the golden leaves green. While we are there, let's glue the leaves that have fallen off back onto the trees. Let us also get some heat lamps to shine out of the skies so that we can believe that we are still in summer. It is possible to achieve this desired outcome through the skilful work of disguise; consider all the mastery we have in creating apps for everything we need and do not need. The missing vital element would be genuine summer, including all of its natural energy and elements. Also, summer could never be authentic without its brilliant transition to autumn. We would never enjoy the incredible beauty of autumn with its unique energy and purpose like providing animals with just a little more foraging time while they prepare for a winter that could be cold and harsh; a winter that also holds in its character a unique purpose.

The important consideration to make regarding the greying of our heads is to examine just who is controlling our standards in liking or not liking this condition. If we choose to colour our grey heads as an expression of our creativity, we rightfully celebrate the will to create. If we choose to keep our grey heads free and wild, we celebrate its will to be part of our creative expression as well.

A distinctive and honest clarification between expression and disguise needs to be made in the politics of transforming grey heads.

In choosing to disguise your grey heads, it is never too late to ask your Self some or all of the following questions, followed by making some affirmations:

What am I hiding?

I have one unique life with multiple destinations for growth. No one destination is identical to another.

What I have lived has passed. Right now, I must dance to the music that is playing!

I look forward while driving in the journey of life because looking back would cause me to drive recklessly.

My one unique life will shine. I know it will because I am consciously living every minute of it.

It is time to reconnect with my inner strength as I go through my transformation into the empowered state of my life.

If my transition feels turbulent, it is never too late to ask for the assistance and support of another conscious individual.

In Living Older, wear your head up high:

Represent your kingdom like a rock star. As long as you are not hurting anyone else or breaking any universal, legal rules, you make the rules of how you express yourself. There is an abundance of choices available in the playing field of individual expression where contradictions are welcome.

Count your choices, because there are many. If you choose to colour your hair, create the mood of your expression and have fun with it. If you choose to wear your grey/silver hair, express its glory like an inherited crown you earned with dutiful pride. Keep your head up and dignified as it walks in tandem with the life you have lived and intend to continue living.

Being 'anti' with ageing signifies that you are 'anti' with Self.

A unique life well lived is incomparable to any other unique life well lived. Its individual beauty has an audience somewhere waiting to be inspired.

Life is not for hiding. Life is for living.

Life is not only for the young. Somewhere in time, a useless and purposeless someone may have started this idea and it spread like wildfire. Only you, the owner of your life are responsible for how you will design your ageing. Whether you choose to wait for the end of life, or wait for the beginning of another new adventure to explore is entirely up to you.

Whatever your choice for life, own the head you wear.

The Grey Area

A Sprinkle of Silver-Shine Questions
and Thoughts

Who is setting the standards for your life?

Who is deciding what is right?

What is wrong with who you need to be?

Are you lacking in anyway that limits you from being of use to at least one other person than yourself? Check-in on the life you are living right now.

Come to terms with the holistic changes you are experiencing, and determine the genuine barriers preventing you from living your life.

Understand the truth that you are still very much alive.

The only excuses that exist are the ones you have created to limit your Self.

The New Grey of Hair

Crazy, Beautiful and Necessary Ideas

Discover your secret super-power as you *Live Older.*

It is never too late to rediscover it or to acknowledge it.

Wear your head like the crown of your kingdom.

Whatever you choose for style, own it.

If your hair is weak, it is time to look into the wellness and health of your body and mind.

If you choose to keep your hair, although it is scanty, design it to suit your look.

Change the style according to your day.

Alternatively, a clean-shaven head is an option for expressive art. It will serve as a unique canvas that can change daily. Hair is hair like nails are nails, the importance lies where we place it.

Exhibit the various designs of grey. There is a whole lot of creative head and hair to be discovered here once the disguising stops.

Choose to not give the disgrace and shaming served by others so much power. Instead, empower Self-cultivated grace, curious fun, and the power of nothing to lose.

A Side Story

I inherited the genes for the premature greying of hair from my very generous ancestors. I began colouring my hair at the age of eighteen. At the time, I tried most hair colours and enjoyed the different looks they provided to match the ever changing shades of my personality. Although I wondered about toxic chemicals that were a part of the ingredients in these colours, I did not yet have sufficient knowledge to take action. When I was thirty-nine and mother to a newly born baby as well as a thirteen year old son, I was diagnosed with a terminal illness. For health reasons, I decided to stop colouring my hair.

Not many people around me knew of my illness. It was however, incredible how many unsupportive comments I received about deciding to remain grey. Some worried that 'the grey' was going to create a negative shift in my life; and some were convinced I was going to look older, a supposedly huge problem because I would begin to look older than the older people around me who were colouring their hair. The remarks got me thinking about how a colour change and the idea of being old without purpose were both easily mixed up, causing confusion.

As my state of health transitioned from terminal to healing from the illness, I continued colouring my hair, but the contradictions concerning the toxicity of the hair colours remained. In hindsight, healing from a huge terminal illness is already a big challenge and a life-changing phenomenon. Yet, I continued to focus on my image and how to look and feel during this time, pointing out the importance that we give to our superficial self-analysis.

Two years later, having recovered, I had come to a firm decision. I was going to leave my hair uncoloured. I was launching a new brand of 'me'. I was given an extension of life, and I was going to wear it proudly. Like any new launch, the new ground of transition was a little wobbly. There was a constant merging of the insecurities between the past me, and the confident new me. This created some not-so-good days as well as some power inducing shifts in my self-transformation. By the end of the second year of leaving my hair uncoloured, my hair began to take on a natural and creative spin of its own design. Spruced by my deep freedom and the courage to do what I knew was the best for my Self, my hair naturally took on a unique design in the shades of silver, grey and a dark-lined crown.

My head is a unique crown; there is an aura that surrounds it because it knows no embarrassment or disguise, contrary to the Anti-Age messages that consciously and unconsciously spread their messages of insecurity around us.

My head is a crown I wear proudly as I stand by my pro-health reasons. As I progressed into my mid-forties, I came to experience that my silver grey crown was making a new and powerful statement, perhaps the statement was always powerful, but my realisation of it was new.

Everywhere I presented myself, my hair either made other people uncomfortable about their choices, or it shone with an aura of my self-confidence as it matched the vibrancy of my soul. The greyness of my hair did not shape the mood of my behaviour. It did not tell me that I was unattractive or uninteresting. What it did was remind me there is never a good enough reason to allow another's judgement or opinion choose how I need to express my individual Self.

I am grateful for this experience because it was never about hair or its colour. Our physical body and mind are designed to deteriorate, bringing into play the art and skill in *Living Older* in complementing the natural process of a natural life.

The natural deterioration of the physical body and the mind does not have a lesser value than the 'much sought after' vibrancy of youth. In completing the decathlon of life, we cannot choose one event to be of more importance than another. This discipline is only gloriously won by completing every phase the best we can without comparison with another.

Embrace the new and mightier phase in life as the seasons in your life change. Here is a phase of life that requires power in Self more than it does in the accumulation of goods. As the body becomes frail, the soul becomes larger. In flowing with the natural design of this process, you will realise material goods of this world can no longer be supported by the body and the mind that are becoming frail with the enlarged weight of the soul. This higher consciousness requires a different high.

I know that I have lived the days of my life savouring each drop of what is given to me. With every new moment that arrives, I know that I am committed to receiving what else comes my way, and in creating what I need from it.

My wild soul will be my guide. I am grateful for the mind, and the body it lives in. As my body changes, it will provide me with non-monotonous, and new challenges in learning creative ways for its care. It is my responsibility to keep my body and mind well and to be in awe of what I receive from them in return. In making a choice to live my life with such passion, I am not missing what has passed and I have no regrets to hold onto as I keep moving forward.

52.
So What's With The Wrinkle Wrapping?

Wrinkles are an individual piece of art that mirrors the story of a lived life.

This is true in *Living Older*. If you have always been a grouch, the wrinkles begin to form a mask of seasoned grouchiness. If you have laughed many a times, the wrinkles begin to form a mask of seasoned laugh lines, minute traces of laughter imprints that once lasted seconds, and now have created a well-deserved and comfortable permanent feature on your face.

Like a thumbprint, every line is an individual and unique piece of work. Taking it away or pretending to erase them is a form of denial of an authentic life that has been yours in the years lived by you. Change is inevitable because our bodies are designed for this change. From the instant we are born, we are changing constantly until we leave our physical bodies behind as we journey on. Why then, do we hold on to the idea of an everlasting youth? Why do we believe that we are cursed with age? Could it be that we are living in limitations set by our Self within the enticing 'Buy-Buy-Buy World'?

In *Living Older*, you will train Self to reach awesomeness when addressing wrinkles. Comparing wrinkles that took years to develop to smoother, taut skin is an idea as useless as saying that babies should remain crawling so that we can 'control' them better lest they start to walk, to run and to go crazy as teens, and finally become adults.

The bullying and the disgracing of wrinkles must stop now.

Replace the aged and non-serving perception that wrinkles are shameful with the idea that they are designs of radical and uncontrollable lines full of free energy. As a bonus, it is never too late to create new lines that reflect a chosen well-lived life on the canvas of our face. There are countless camouflaging effects available because the demand for this abuse is prevalent. There is a lot of energy and money spent in developing better and better methods for this camouflage in order to market the idea that looking older is a shameful event that needs to be hidden or ironed out!

What the farfallas!

Eyes that twinkle and have a curious mischief in them do not fade, especially when nourished with life-enhancing foods. Wrinkles enveloping these eyes create an outstanding contrast between the everlasting energy of the experienced wild soul that shines through them in a physical body that has been well used for a great service. These eyes have always been alive and continue to be (even if behind glasses) ready to catch an opportunity for curiosity that flies by. No matter the age, these eyes are never dead eyes.

Wrinkles on my face do not translate to a negative outcome of my life. The negative outcome of my life would occur if I realised that I was collecting frown wrinkles or misery-laden wrinkles, or sad, regretful wrinkles that had been permanently etched on my face as a reflection of the stories I missed in living my life. They would be a reminder of a life I did not live, or one I could have chosen to live, certainly a life of constant regret and dissatisfaction. It would make sense to hide these types of lines, but it is not the life I want, so I have to live the life I want by design.

The more you live consciously, the more you will collect lines of all colours and varieties. These will represent your interactive actions of moments well lived, both in dark times and lighter times.

I will collect the edgier lines and the cuddlier ones. I will be very conscious of how often I smile in a day: big, natural smiles that are free to stretch and relax on my face as the joy from inside my soul accompanies life on its journey with no discriminations.

Pay attention to how our environment is filled with messages about how we must look, always telling us that we are never good enough at any phase in our life. We are surrounded by noise that tells us to add the prefix 'anti' before our naturally ageing selves. When the Self is unconscious, it has insecurities that respond to the messages telling us to hide our wrinkles. Why do we heed to this message? We watch movies about people who are younger and more vibrant. How many younger more vibrant people do we see around us? Most people today are too tired and numb, and they are growing older before their time.

If we do not allow strangers with not-so-good intentions into our house, why do we allow strangers into our personal space to dictate our likes and our dislikes? Then again, when we are numb and unconscious, all invasive procedures are possible. Why do I need to put myself up on a forum to see how many thumbs up or thumbs down I get? Bad days are welcome even if I do not agree to them at the given moment. But when they have passed, I am left with a larger stretch of my Self tested and tried by life and its many transitions.

Perhaps it is because we forget the power of loving our Self. Maybe it is the images and the stories made to entertain us that leave potent time bombs of toxic thought within us. We are exposed to images and stories that encourage us to be in neediness of each other rather than to be in complement with each other. No matter who we are, being liked or loved by everyone is not possible.

When you love your Self, there is no desperate need to look for many other people to love you.

Where are all of the stories that are told by very interesting older people? There must be interesting older people who exist among us.

There is a vital difference between needing another person for the purpose of filling the empty void left by a lack in appreciation of Self and a need to connect with another unique soul in an exchange of meaningful purpose.

I know that there are more lessons to learn on my life journey, however long it lasts. Meanwhile, I will be wearing my life on my face. I will wear my wrinkles one story at a time. Will you join me?

How To Wear Your Life On Your Face

A Few Starting Suggestions

1. Place your Self in as many simple, adventures that celebrate the authenticity of life as possible.

2. Learn as much as you can about your Self in each newly found adventure.

3. Wear the lessons you learn in the adventures of the life you live on your face.

4. Be in the silence of Self.

5. Be aware of each segment of life as it happens.

6. Allow your face to taste freedom as it stretches far in laughter, in awe and in all of life's wonders.

7. Add to your presence. Warning: This may lead to a new and cool condition known as **experiential allure.**

8. 'Talk the Walk' less and 'Walk the Talk' more.

9. Celebrate wrinkles with stories.

10. Design laugh wrinkles in your spare time.

11. Be aware of the everyday emotions that are designing your wrinkles.

12. Be true to your Self no matter what happens, no matter who comes and who goes. Your Self is you and it will always be you.

53.
Eating
To A
Different
Beat

Food is fuel.

Optimal quality food is optimal quality fuel for the many adventures in life that you will continue to have in *Living Older*. Knowledge of the chemistry of digestion and assimilation of this fuel is a pro-life necessity. It is knowledge that belongs to every human individual, as much as knowing that one needs sleep to function. There is no reason to conduct a study in confirming this truth because you live it everyday.

Here is a revelation — matching a way of eating and the type of food you choose to the current tune of the life being lived is a strategic 'street smart-ness' we all need. However, as an individual who is *Living Older*, I know that I am unique, and as a holistic nutritionist, I know that there is no one-way to eat. This means that there is no 'one size fits all' strategy to fit everyone's uniqueness, both internally and externally of the body and mind.

The quest for the perfect food and the perfect diet run in partnership with the never ending quest for the perfect looking body and mind.

In my experience of studying different foods and different ways of exercise as a professional, I am only beginning to understand that as perfect as any one thing or one way of eating can be, it will not remain perfect forever. As a conscious, creative being, I have both a wide expression for dress and the ability to blend in a crowd, should I feel the need. The foods I need are as varied as the many colourful vibes I am living at any time in my life.

Food is fuel. Sometimes, you need more of it and sometimes, you need less of it. Most often, your current emotions affect your food choices. Your present thoughts and actions, your immediate environment and your lack or abundance at any given moment of your life will also influence your decisions concerning food choices. The chemistry of the digestive system of each individual is also different. Food and its reactive chemistry is a different one for each individual. Dietary solutions designed for a large collective are not able to satisfy the individual attention required for each person's unique constitution as well as life story.

The original and self-sustaining source of food is provided to us by Nature. It is designed to be intricately complex so that those who need a quick fix will not find a solution. Alternatively, those who cultivate patience and consciousness will gain not just from its nourishing gifts but also from its contagious qualities of respect, connection and perseverance in living the life of Self, while remaining connected to others.

Our state of numbness, initiates our continuing ignorance concerning our food sources. The missing consciousness regarding food, our source for survival, has allowed for its easy manipulation that has allowed our planet to become dis-eased and stressed with toxicity.

Food is life. Optimal quality of our food source leads to an optimal quality of life. Natural, whole foods and animals love for their freedom to be connected to the laws of Nature. The unequivocal energy we get in the presence of Nature is what plants and animals get too. Keeping our foods real and in tune with Nature is as necessary as it is for us to have the right to live a life. We are living longer, but we are also surrounded by many illnesses and disease. We accept that our landfills are overflowing, just as easily as we accept that it is normal for our digestive systems to be clogged.

Nature's beautiful unspoilt soil, which could be used to grow more trees for oxygen, and more fruit trees and plants for food, is being stuffed with man-made toxic garbage that Nature cannot digest and put to good use. Similarly, we eat quick and easy food with little thought to how our body digests it. The knowledge of food is not limited to what we eat and how much we eat. It is about what is digested and how it is digested.

When you allow your awareness to awaken, you become the only expert there is concerning your digestion.

Any other expert you go to for assistance, when your digestion is in trouble, will still have to ask you questions about what is happening inside of you. When you eat clean and real foods provided by Nature, your digestive system knows how to function to the maximum potential of its design. At the same time you will have less plastic packaging that gets thrown back to Nature, your life's source.

The health of the planet is connected to, and affected by, the garbage thrown back at it while our eyes fixate on screens that entertain our numb states, and our minds are unconscious to its consequences. This form of garbage benefits nothing 'with life', and it will forever accumulate for our future generations as a legacy of our selfish, rude and inconsiderate ways.

When I eat clean, I put out clean. When I eat processed artificial foods, my digestion is clogged, my brain is fogged and my body starts to store waste products from chemical reactions it does not understand.

We often believe that being older is equal to being sick. But being sick is not a normal part of *Living Older*. The idea of sickness as a requirement to growing older is more relevant to the case of 'my cup runneth over' from life choices already lived in the history of one's life. In this context, the toxins and non-vital foods you eat and accumulate in your system during the entirety of your life will equal the worth in its investment as you become older.

Eating foods that do not serve in optimising your Self is like putting poor quality fuel in a perfect and beautifully engineered car.

What it could feel like in body and mind:

> 1st stage - lethargy, brain fog (dull mind), constipation, bloating, fat build-up, lack of energy, a congested appearance such as puffy eyes and blocked sinuses.
> 2nd stage - undigested foods, distended intestines, gluey blood, distorted blood cells, aching muscles and joints.
> 3rd stage - lack of nourishment for our vital organs, thick and sticky blood, narrowed vessels, sick and abnormal cells.

Real foods come from the same source of wisdom that feeds us with each breath we take to live—Nature. Real foods provide us with the nutrients we need to function at optimal levels as we live a life. The rich and well-balanced nutrients come from the soil from which it grows. If the soil is toxic from man-made concoctions and inconsiderate waste, the nutrients will include the toxicity but not the vibrant energy it is designed to provide for us.

Real food has a natural SWITCH-OFF button integrated into it. For example, you love broccoli. You really love broccoli! If you were allowed an unlimited amount of raw or slightly cooked broccoli to eat, you would stop when your body has reached the saturating point for what the broccoli is offering your body. It will be almost impossible to force yourself to keep eating it.

Now let us continue our little experiment by replacing the broccoli with a bag of potato crisps that required human intervention to make it. Processed foods such as chips, are designed to feed your cravings. Like addictive drugs, you get hooked, wanting more and more. Our bodies keep accepting these empty foods because the switch-off button is not designed to recognise any of the artificial ingredients in these foods, so we continue to 'stuff ourselves' until we start to feel sick.

Seek live rhythms in the quality of foods you choose to eat.

In *Living Older*, you acknowledge the duration of a life is a part of the magical unknown. However, while you are consciously alive, you need to relearn the value of food and its chemistry in order to keep you functioning at your optimal best. You need to relearn to get in touch with your place in, and your partnership with, Nature. You need to reconnect with respecting its inherent wisdom.

I intend to function in harmony with the rhythm of the Universe and in the laws of Nature as I live my journey in life. A vital component in realising my intention is in being consciously aware of eating to a different beat.

May I invite you to do the same?

Food Chemistry and The Unique You

A Sprinkle of Questions in Awareness to Ask Your Self

1. Does what goes in to your body's digestive system come out at the end of this well-designed system?

2. Is there excess mucous excreted from your body minutes or hours after you eat a certain food or meal?

3. Does your mind feel disconnected and uninterested after eating certain foods?

4. Is there itchiness on the skin, inside your throat, the genital areas, the bum, the nose, the eyes?

5. Do you become overly sensitive?

6. Is the food you want to eat the only thing on your mind? Can you replace it with something else?

7. Do you slow down and become sleepy or lethargic after eating a certain food or a meal?

8. Does the food you eat add energy or remove energy from you?

9. Do your joints feel sensitive?

10. Do your muscles hurt?

11. Do you feel acid coming up into your mouth?

12. Is your tongue thickly coated and mouth smelly when you wake up in the morning?

13. Are you full of gas? Not the helium kind! The kind that makes you fart and burp leaving people around you unfairly intoxicated.

14. Do your eyes or your nose water in the morning?

15. Are you out of breath when you run or walk up the stairs or a slope?

16. Is food making you feel emotionally better, or worse?

Eating to a Different Beat

A Sprinkle of Ideas

1. Choose to eat foods as an investment to life rather than choose foods for its bankruptcy.

2. Be aware of your unique digestion and assimilation processes.

3. Be quality strong and quantity low in food choices.

4. Eat real food grown from soil that follows the laws of Nature, not the laws of mankind.

5. Buy foods with very little packaging that can be reused or recycled.

6. Know every ingredient in the foods that you choose to eat. The less there are the better it is.

7. Eat what Nature provides in the environment you live, geographically and seasonally.

8. Drink water that is clean and without chemicals like clean spring water or re-energised distilled water.

9. Check whether you are feeding the 'noise' or feeding the soul.

10. Remember this: 'I do to myself as I do to my planet'.

11. Learn strategic eating - one that suits your many rhythms and adventures.

12. Try on the idea of eating less and eating smart. We are overfed and undernourished.

13. Move forward without sugar. Stop spending too much energy on looking at it like it is an enemy or something bad. Instead, observe if it is serving you to better function in the long-term.

14. It is time to zone in on the ownership of your body and consciousness. Ask yourself: 'Do I feel good'? 'How do I regain the control in understanding my body's language'?

15. Notice if you are tired or develop a tendency to be numbed after eating certain foods. This could be a side-effect due to poor assimilation of foods, or due to insufficient beneficial nutrients from real foods.

16. Identify who owns your body.

17. Whatever you eat, be aware of it as it enters your body. Be conscious of its effects on your body and mind after it has passed the senses of your mouth. Observe if it has an exit plan.

18. Use the awareness and wisdom of your body in any situation, environment, and time as the '**Chief Approval Officer**' for what goes into your body, and why it is allowed to go in.

19. Know that everyone's body and mind are unique to them. Your reactions are affected by personal immersions into the varying environments of your life, which include both the celebrations and the sorrows that come with each one of these life experiences.

Food, wellness, nutrition and the care of our mind and body are sinking under the weight of so much information. Everyone seems to be an expert on what is good versus what is not good. I have consciously decided not to include more food-related wisdom here.

Instead, I invite you to join an event, or workshop, which we have organised with specific themes, for a more focused assistance and guidance in the necessary art and science of food its many uses for our wellbeing.

54.
Keep
The Muscles
Flexible And
Pulled Back

My body and mind have always been attracted to movement and being involved with sports was the most natural means in acquiring this high.

As the years continued, I was not too interested in team sports, but my love for movement never left. My wild soul just loves to move. Even if I ask it to remain still for a moment, my soul will dance in the sparkle of my eyes.

Walking is the first and the most adventurous form of movement. The environment or the scenario is never the same. The route you take, even the same route, is different each time. The ability to move from a sitting position allows for much activity within the body. Writing this book has been a great test and a challenge in exploring other ways of writing outside of sitting! A moving body is like a stream. It's full of self-generated energy.

In *Living Older*, there is no competition in movement. There is and always will be another good reason to move in tune to a rhythmic beat—the breath. The breath is the rhythm of life you carry within Self. Whenever movement takes place in conditions where the soul is present, there is deep and immense pleasure and contentment. When movement takes place in an environment that is rigorous, the body works towards its result, but the soul is absent. This does not mean that there is a discrimination against rigorous exercise. What remains most important is how movement or exercise best serves you—the individual. We are conditioned to believe there are only a limited number of ways to move for benefit.

We need different flavours of movement at anytime.

In *Living Older*, both the body and the mind need to move. You can learn to identify what movement best connects with Self at different times of need. The only condition driving the movement you choose is how much awareness and care you learn to reinvest into your holistic body, and not just the separated inventory of its parts.

We live in a culture that promotes long hours of sitting. If you spend long hours of sitting at work, or in creating your craft, balance the sitting with pockets of movement immediately.

Movement

A Stretch of Ideas

Walk anywhere and everywhere. Walk short or long, near or far, rain or shine.

Stretch your body and mind in rhythm with breath. You will cultivate a natural reminder not to be stationary, whether you are sitting on a chair while reading or eating, standing in a queue, lying in bed before sleeping, and at any other time. No excuses.

Create rhythmic movements with your body to your favourite music.

Make use of weight-bearing opportunities for the muscles in your body.

Perform movements that encourage the deep inhalation of oxygen and the strong exhalation of carbon dioxide.

Match the rhythmic movements of another human being in play and pleasure.

Movement

Key Areas

Soul

Neck

Shoulders

Eyes

Jaw

Valuable small areas between the Vertebrae of the Spine

Postural muscles. Small and extremely relevant to the foundation of our presence.

Joints

Digestive system

Energy points in our Body and Mind Toes, Fingers and all their 'in-betweeners'

Breath

Mind

Voice

Curiosity

Be aware of the effects of movement within each area. Check with your medical practitioner before any exercise or exertion in movement.

55.
Touch And Be Touched By Presence

Touching someone by your presence is a valuable lesson that may take a lifetime to learn.

The beauty of being human is in the continuous discovery of the many innate values we have, especially when we become enlightened with our 'increased years'. We recognise the existence of both good and bad within us, and we begin to be more comfortable living life with the unknown choices we will make.

We have created many fictional scenarios of heroes and courageous beings. It is only in true action, however, where you will discover what you are able to do, or not to do. If each of our uniqueness were celebrated, we would have a priceless wealth of inspiration from which to pull from at any time that we require some encouragement and motivation in living life. You will have an urge to unlock your gaze from the stories on a screen in exchange for real stories that you create, or stories you are inspired by when in the presence of many different real people.

It is time to *Live Older* by using your presence in the service of another. Often we understand this means to volunteer or to give freely of ourselves, but this is not what I mean in this context. You can give of your Self through a business you create, or the crafted work you create. You can give of your Self through the art and entertainment you provide. You can give priceless wealth with a heartfelt smile and a hug and with a hand you extend in care.

Share a smile even when no one smiles back at you. Give a hand with the groceries, or assist one who clearly needs it without the Self-gratification of a 'Thank You'. Give a greeting without expecting a response. A kind word equals rocket fuel to the person in need of it. Strike up a good conversation and/or give a heart-to-heart hug. Just because! The ability to love unconditionally and fearlessly is done without expectation.

If your emotions get hurt, feel the pain.

In *Living Older*, realise that focusing on the pursuit of self-gain for contentment is a bottomless pit. You can continue in its search for a long time, but it will always be out of your reach. The ability to interconnect with other souls is a quick shortcut for lessons in the real meaning of life.

Touching someone with your presence happens without a calculated benefit.

Accept that you will be touched in the presence of another being, too. Giving alone creates a serious imbalance when you are not receiving the many invisible gifts offered to you everyday. You will give your senses 'something to talk about' as you travel the life you live. Be afraid only of what you have not tried, and only for a while.

Please note, in the context of the book, I am referring only to people you are familiar with in relationship, work or community. Before extending of your presence physically with hugs and love, ensure the presence of both your consciousness and your intuition so that you are attuned with the intentions or the wariness of the recipient.

Be grateful to be sensually alive. Be openly touched by the presence of another human being and their unique soul.

Continuous Learning, Support and Community

Could It Be?

We start to design life,
young and restless
having spent so much time writing and reading,
now ready and open to promised possibilities,
risks, opportunities and invincibility.
Our objectives for freedom
lie in material purpose
leading us quickly into the illusion
of finances and
more and more of it
in order to satisfy our fast growing needs and wants
led farther and farther away
from the original purpose we set out to find.
We work and we work
to satisfy them one by one.
We tag ourselves successful or unsuccessful.
Others will look up or they will look down.
Time quickly passes.
Conscious purpose becomes so blurred
and very hard to find.
Possibilities seem absent.
Change is suffocated by fear.
We need love,
whatever it looks like.
There is none available
for Self.
Alone is sad

because everyone said so.
'A half a person to be with is much better than none'
they said.
Partners, children and friends
accumulate.
Soon
we begin
to take all for granted
because it is so much easier.
Purpose of Self is still nowhere to be found
'Rocking the boat' may leave us alone.
Again
Alone is sad
because everyone said so.
Fear is there, too,
more of it now.
Fear of failing.
Fear of making a fool of myself.
I need the applause.
Where is what I was promised?
The illusion I realise now was illusive.
Soon
my body is changing.
I can change too.
The many years gathered
to be what I have been told to be.
If I do not move now
If I sit calmly and wait
no one will realise
I too, once had
promised possibilities, risks, opportunities and invincibility.
Freedom.
My purpose.

10

What Is, but Can Not Continue to Be

What I write is only the tip of an iceberg that is staring us in the face. It is an iceberg deeply rooted in the design of life as we have it today. Embracing the phase of our 'increased years' is of importance to all of us, no matter our age. We just refuse to see it. As long as we can sense life, acknowledging death as a natural part of its completion is a vital and urgent component in living a purposeful life. No one person's life has a guaranteed life span. No one, no matter the quantity of accumulated power or material wealth, knows their exact time of separation from their earthly body.

In choosing to consciously *Live Older*, you have a personal design to create for living. It has to be individually tested and tried for size. There is nothing in it that is a one-size-fits-all. The years available for *Living Older* are a blessing, never to be misunderstood as a curse. If we were gifted a long life, we can either wait each hour and day for time to pass or we could redesign the extended time to create an entirely new way of being that is different from any previous way of living our lives. Herein, we will discover genuine excitement, purpose and many more reasons for celebration. Life at any phase, when designed authentically considers the needs and the references of the current 'Now' for each different individual. *Living Older* is not a lifestyle that begins at any chronological age. It is a way to live from the very beginning in the circle of life.

Today, the view on ageing is a limited one, with a bias towards negativity, which has been brewed from years of habit, thought and perception. To be older is to have an extended opportunity to shine your bright light, and it is not a curse or something that must be shrouded with dread. The positive results that exist with increasing age can only be available when we personally implement effective practices in awareness and in the wellness of Self.

Is there a guarantee to how your body and mind will function up until 'the finale'? No, because such a knowledge remains a part of the mysterious unknown. The only available truth is the power to own the life you are living right at this moment. This moment includes all the ups and the downs that come your personal way and the choices you will make in living them. The ability to look after your Self with awareness and increased consciousness, along with the capacity to create positive change, will assist you in choosing a path that leads to more natural and positive outcomes.

Our way of life today is centred in working for money. Such a focus can make us numb to every other sensibility we have. The designed process of this quest for overwhelming material wealth involves moving down a conveyor belt from one predetermined phase of life to another: hospitalised birth, day care, kindergarten, school, university, job, career, marriage, kids, a mortgage and retirement. Eventually, we remove the old who are no longer players in the field; and therefore, are no longer useful in this system. Because the aged are mostly classified as dependent, they are left to live in homes while they wait for their unknown date of death. We repeat this cycle by bringing up our children to learn the same lessons.

This design in living divides our lives according to blocks of monetary importance, rather than creating a circular and interconnected life.

The journey of life, like a ride on a Ferris wheel, is a continuous circular ride that provides you with a different view all of the time, each a different one with none comparable to the other. This is a life by design, yet it is not the only available design for life. The design can be re-created and tailored to fit a life of *Living Older*.

We need to begin a review of the systems and processes around ageing. Living a life requires courage, love and compassion, mixed with mistakes and lots of dark and light shades. Any illusion of 'happily ever after' is purely fictional. The last chapters of any life are always available for a turnaround in order to become of valuable importance. It is never too late. As long as you can breathe, life runs in you. We must not accept any category of life to exist without purpose.

What the farfallas!

It is little wonder no one wants to grow old. It is time to clearly differentiate between the 'older' which means living a way of being that does not serve again and again and again and the other 'older' which means a person with increased age.

It is time to reinstate the superpower and wisdom of the elder. By practicing to *Live Older*, these traits will become more accessible as effective problem solvers in acquiring an active consciousness, in being of positive evolution, in continuous learning, and in empowerment of the Self, not focusing on age as a number but in living a life of constant purpose.

Seek the bright-eyed spirit shining out of a being full of rich stories that spring from where action is bigger than talk.

Yearn for the magnetic attraction of curiosity and free energy that exude out of a big life that is continuing to live like a great book that is hard to put down.

It is a time to live and to remain alive. It is a time to learn so many lessons. It is a time for so much more to do. Start with conversations about it—open, exciting conversations.

Start *Living Older*.

Immediately.

What If Older Was Meant To Be Sublimely Awesome

*What if
it was an embrace
of warm light
in turning towards
the later and later
years of life.
A light that
switched on the consciousness
that brought in the calm
from rowing in the material world.
It turned up the volume
of a possibility for newness
for a curiosity to live.
To be
the best that
we can be
in connection
to all else.
Perhaps,
it would be
sublimely*
AWESOME

ON A TOUS VÉCU

We did it all.

11

Revitalised Perspectives in Ageing

A Brief Guide To Get Started

Practice *Living Older* instead of growing older.

Explore the priority of the Soul. What is the purpose of its visit in this life? How does it feel to you?

Review the current state of your physical body. Are you consciously aware of how it operates? How it reacts to the foods you eat? How it reacts to your environment? What are your standards for its wellbeing? Do you own an awareness scale?

Review the current state of your mind the one that drives thoughts, memories, and hard drive. Do you understand how it operates? Are you in control of the mind or is the mind controlling you?

Live the life you want by designing it. Are you embodying frustration as you continue to live your life according to the standards of another?

Allow your Self to evolve constantly. Do not limit it to comparisons and restrictions; instead, allow it to extend it with opportunities to reach its authentic potential in the choices you make in living your life.

Own Self fully as you Live Older. Am I ready to be conscious and stronger in my being? Will I learn to adapt to change with amazement rather than frustration and despair?

Let us begin to think of better solutions for care that adds to a life, not one that subtracts from a life.

Honour the importance of being surrounded and enveloped by the ones who love you. Include all who have shared life with you, such as family, friends and community. Always make room for new relationships.

If love from others is not available to you, design new environments for your Self where you include others who need love and care in a shared community.

Alienation from family and community are not to be considered as acceptable solutions for care of the elderly. In *Living Older*, a community will be designed with all the unique sounds and energy of people of different ages intermingling with each other to provide the balance of life. It must never be acceptable to remove an individual from their life space.

The 'I' in the individual does not expire until the soul has moved on in the continuous journey of life.

Being in the company of silence of despair, and of others waiting to pass does not seem to be a fitting finale for a life, any life.

There are many beautiful souls who make it their life's work to care for the aged. However, like everything else in the systems we create, it is a job. Some do it exceptionally and others do not. How do we reconsider the design of this important requirement?

Seek adventure endlessly—the kind that is healthy and legal.

12

A Recipe for Making Living Older a Whole Lot Cooler

1. Take a bowl full of magic of the unknown.

2. Replace fear of death with fear of not living to the best of your conscious ability.

3. Add drops of adventures never too late to experience.

4. Marinate all in the love you have for others, including lives you have touched and lives that have touched you.

5. Fine-tune the recipe several times while making your life a meaningful one for others, and for the planet that is temporarily your home.

Sage*, Licorice Root*, Mint*, Fennel*

Perhaps The Tea that Wise'ths Thee .

* Always the highest quality from Nature and no one else..

"Place right hand over left hand. Thumbs lightly pressed over the weblike space between the index finger and thumb on both hands. Place hands over centre of chest and relax".

Perhaps The Points that Calm'eth Thee .

* Always be one in mind, body and spirit with Nature and no one else

The labels within the illustration read:

*Coconut Milk or Coconut Water or Water

*Vanilla Paste fresh from Pod

*Cacao Powder

*Cardamom Seeds from Pod

*Sweeten according to personal beliefs

1. Chill until just starting to freeze
2. Blend and Enjoy Chilled. Be in *Gratitude for your *Life

Perhaps The Drink that Alive'ns Thee .

*Always the highest quality from Nature and no one else..

* Basil *essential oil 4 drops*

Lemon essential oil 4 Drops

Peppermint essential oil 5 drops

Neroli essential oil 3 drops

*In 15ml of *Coconut Oil*

Perhaps The Fix that Alert'ens Thee .

Always use the 100% pure and most sustainable from Nature and no one else

* *Neroli*
  6 drops

* *Spruce*
  5 drops

* *Sandalwood*
  4 drops

* *Myrrh*
  4 drops

* *Tangerine*
  6 drops

* *Cinnamon*
  4 drops

* *Geranium*
  5 drops

in *Jojoba or *Sweet Almond Oil

Perhaps The Oil that Pleasure'th Thee .

*Always use the 100% pure and most sustainable from Nature and no one else

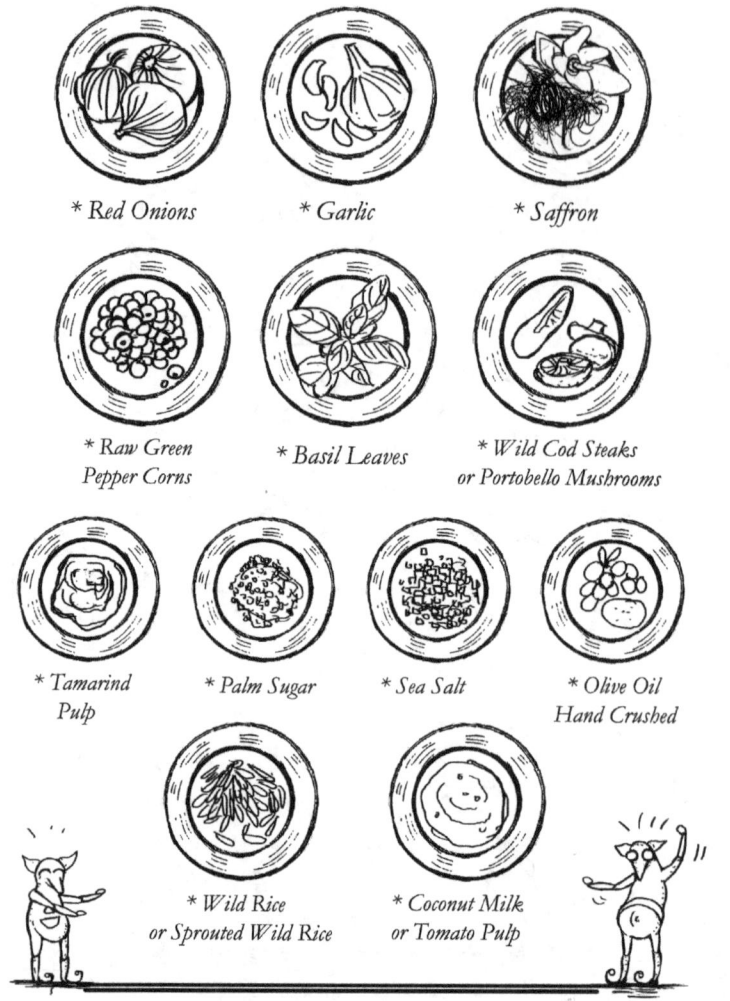

* Red Onions

* Garlic

* Saffron

* Raw Green
Pepper Corns

* Basil Leaves

* Wild Cod Steaks
or Portobello Mushrooms

* Tamarind
Pulp

* Palm Sugar

* Sea Salt

* Olive Oil
Hand Crushed

* Wild Rice
or Sprouted Wild Rice

* Coconut Milk
or Tomato Pulp

"Bring these ingredients together the best way it suits you"

Perhaps The Pot of Forever Love To Connect'eth Thee .

*Always use the 100% pure and most sustainable from Nature and no one else

Change-Inducing Ideas for Living Older

An Action Plan to Start Immediately

Create a new business using the craft of your hands as a product. Learn how to do this.

Refuse to take part in anti-ageing. By taking part, you are encouraging the shut down of a time of heightened consciousness from Self, from community and from mankind. This creates an imbalance on the planet and it serves those who wish to take advantage of it.

Join the WOWAGEING™ Movement and learn to *Live Older*. Be supported and guided as we move forwards in creating positive change in our Self, and in mankind.

Extend and build connections and relationships of purpose with intermingling generations, not segregated ones.

Celebrate life in preparing for death.

Eat foods that give you life, not death.

Learn to be uncomfortable, often.

Affirm, accept and live that every living being is growing everyday. This is a natural law, no matter what you are told to believe.

Live now, not tomorrow.

In a world where change is rapid, make active choices instead of passive ones.

Keep your personal awareness sharp and available at all times.

Create playgrounds or playtime for natural highs.

Implement daily platforms for creative expression in *Living Older*. Rock it big time!

Cultivate your wild soul.

Fall in love every day with the gift of your life.

Find gratitude at every five breaths you take.

While you rejoice at your newfound youth and the illusive freedom it provides you, let me venture forth into exploring new adventures that come with completing a life well lived.

I will keep moving towards the magical mystery of the unknown with my life pack full of the very freedom I gained, and the experiences I dared because I lived every moment as if it was the only one.

14

Preparing The Finale of a Unique and Grand Life

My life is a theatrical masterpiece, a one-of-a-kind performance. Throughout each session of the performance, I have been alive with excitement, sadness, anxiety, worry, passion, love and immense gratitude. I will continue to be alive, even as my body and my mind prepare for the expiration of serving my soul in this chapter of my existence.

I am already eternally grateful. My life is exciting because I designed it for my Self. It is proof that I pushed against the edges of comfort to attain a larger life. It is an imperfect life that I cherish. It is not waiting to be approved by another's standards. *Living Older* is about feverishly writing a life story while we live it until the very end.

A heart-lived story of another being's life is what I want to hear. I am not interested in the whiny regret about what was not accomplished. I want to hear outrageous stories about growing older that are accompanied by a permanent smile imprinted as wrinkles on a face.

When I choose to Live Older, I am guaranteed death in the midst of truly living my life.

My wild soul wants to be on the stage that I designed, performing my life with great supporting props and supporting characters, with whom I would have shared important connections and purpose. They will continue to acknowledge my role as the main character in the award-winning story called my life.

When my bones, skin, hair and grey matter regress and start to shut down according to the laws that gave me this beautiful life, I will still be in gratitude. I will not pretend to be unafraid as the changes accelerate; after all, I was born into an era of free speech that allowed for the 'full surround-sound effect' of the media's messages to encourage the blatant resonances of fear and self-doubt in us, and to influence what we thought we were required to be.

Death is as natural as living. If life is truly beautiful, why will I be afraid of death? I live with my head up, looking forwards as I journey the rest of my life creating priceless stories, and marking every moment of my existence. This is the only acknowledgement of value that I can make with my final breath.

This period of fear and uncertainty will pass because I will have learned so much by having my consciousness in communication with my soul. My enlightened soul will celebrate a fully owned life, lived with a sense of presence and beauty that served my mind well in the physical house of my body. My life includes all the grit and frustrations, the likes and the dislikes, mixed in with all the beautiful rainbow sparkles of joyous wonderment. It is a life that will include experiences both right and wrong that are a result of extending my Self out from the safe perimeters of a comfortable zone of my own making. I will laugh at the mistakes I make because they bring my soul unexpected adventures that I never would have known existed.

On the stage of 'my finale', I will go out with an overwhelming applause for my life and its entire journey. I will have no regrets for taking ownership of the life I have, and the one I lived. I will take a grand bow as I leave the stage and bid farewell to all the people with whom I have had the honour to know. Perhaps in way of return, I stirred, and even tickled, their lives. My wild soul will soar with pride when it leaves my physical body and journeys on to the next stage of this awesome experience called 'the uncertain life'.

Bravo! Bravo! Bravo!

My Wild Soul and I

*I got to know my soul
when I was about five or six years old.
I did not know right then that it was my soul or the essence of who I am.*

*I would talk to myself in silence.
Share the troubles of my growing up years.
I know, only now, that it was my soul I was talking to
because it felt good to be in communication with it.*

*My soul soothed me when I was alone and scared.
It prodded me on with confidence
when I wanted to do something
I felt strongly in my gut I needed to do.*

*I was a little girl then.
Now, I am a grown woman.*

*My body is changing but my soul has not.
It has only become a more clear and
conscious part of who I am and what I do.*

*I know that my body is the house of my soul.
It will weather as the journey in my life continues.
This is only natural to me.
My soul has not weathered.*

It is shinier and bolder than it was when I recognised it at six years old.
I know this because my conversations with my soul have not changed.
They are more vivacious than ever.

We have created so many stories together,
my soul and I.
We have more to live as we continue in our journey of life.

It is my responsibility to assist my body and mind
to keep up with my very large soul.
My body is a gift for the use of Now.
My soul takes the journey of life I sow.

It is my soul that guides me to how I live.
My body comes along for the ride.
Its care is the best interest of my soul and I.
Its care is my responsibility and no one else's.

I look around me.
I see that I am not alone.
There are others who know this.
There are many who have forgotten.

Maybe, it was different
for them.

This is how my soul and I choose to live.
I offer its thoughts
to others who need a reminder
that what is priceless
already is in deep within.

WOWAGEING™
An Introduction

A concept for The Art of Living Older.

It is at the infant stage of its concept.

A positive movement that includes a worldwide community of like-minded people who are committed to replace growing older with *Living Older.*

Abides by the 55 evolvers presented in this book and it offers assistance to you in the journey of *Living Older.*

Elaborates on the deeper understanding of stumbling blocks that will be encountered in the process of transformation from growing older to *Living Older.*

Its objectives are young with plenty of healthy imperfections, but its intentions are mighty and most importantly, it is powered by wild souls.

Support is provided within the categories of activities, information, and resources.

Coaching for individuals and group sessions will be available depending on scheduled events.

Themed events, both live and online, will be created throughout a calendar year to take place in various parts of the world in the form of workshops, webinars and travel retreats to provide sensual experiences for continuous learning, sharing and curiosity.

What You Need To Do:

1. Visit wowageing.com for further information and for conversations about the book.

2. Join The Community at wowageing.com as a member. Our community is full of purpose, energy, fun and celebrations of all that is imperfect, unknown and alive in *Living Older.*

3. Be a vital part of the community's growth in creating new paths as we choose to *Live Older* rather than grow older. As the days of our living years increase, we have the gift of being of mighty purpose more than ever before.

4. As a member, receive more information concerning special themed events, workshops, courses and travels that will further elaborate how to make the practices work for the individual or groups of people.

WOWAGEING™ Objectives

1. To start a movement in *Living Older* instead of growing older.

2. To create a community of like-minded people in *Living Older*.

3. To elaborate on the understanding of the evolvers during special events, sessions and workshops held both online and live.

4. To explore daring actions for living the best unique life possible, as we continue to *Live Older.*

5. To provide healthy, legal and crazy ideas for change as we begin to live better and more consciously.

6. To create opportunities to nurture The Art of Living Older.

7. To create events for laughter.

8. To celebrate age as it increases.

9. To reinstate the super-powers of the elders.

10. To create strategic systems of positive change to allow for *Living Older.*

11. To create purposeful and positive change in all areas of natural transformations that accompany increased age so that it matches the needs of conscious human beings of value.

12. To end the shaming in being older by choosing to *Live Older.*

WOWAGEING™
Tools & Attitudes

1. Ownership of a **wild soul.**

2. A very open mind.

3. Read *Once Upon A Time I Would Grow Old*, the book.

4. The will to be alive as you live every new day.

5. Crazy courage to 'walk away from the herd'.

6. The ability to learn to walk the talk.

7. A gratitude for your unique Self.

8. An intuitive calling to keep learning.

9. An acceptance that you cannot know everything.

10. Unafraid to be human.

11. Ready for a laugh.

12. The ability to make the mistakes that will bring you forward.

13. Become a global community member at: wowageing.com

Start anything serious by laughing at your Self.

JOIN THE COMMUNITY AT WOWAGEING.COM

WOWAGEING™
The Art of Living Older.

Wild souls, you are not alone. A new movement in *Living Older* has begun!

"It is time to bring out your unique sheep-ness!"

WOWAGEING™ Live & Online Themed Events

WOWAGEING™ conducts events and courses in The Art of Living Older including inspirations and ideas from *Once Upon A Time I Would Grow Old*. You will experience each evolver with your senses in real time while interacting with a larger community of like-minded people in a fun environment. The events will also provide opportunities to dive deep into each individual evolver.

We will be travelling through different countries to launch the book and to conduct events that will take on different forms such as webinars and live talks, travel retreats, two-day workshops both online and live and continuous community support and information for *Living Older*. At the events, there will be recommended tools, ideas, shared food (only available at some live events), laughter and a sense of community.

In writing the book, I made a conscious choice not to address specific and very important age-related conditions for well-being because of the multi-level differences in each of us as individuals. However, what is limited in a book can be made available during live and online sessions. During these live speaking events, I will be able to connect with you more profoundly concerning specialised topics such as food, wellness and creating an individualised strategic design for *Living Older* the best we can.

Topics of Interest to be included in Workshops:

Self-Centred Wellness

The Art and Consciousness of Eating

Food Choices for Nurturing the Mind

Dancing with the Soul

Seeking Opportunities for Conscious Sustenance through Entrepreneurship

Exploring the Process of **Resexatation**™

Creating the Self-Designed Environment

Relearning the Art of Being Silly in order to Save Your Soul

The Never-Ending Guide for the Journey towards the Unknown

Connect With Me

Dear Reader,

Thank you for choosing to read this book. I have for the longest time believed that I am an exceptional being. This is mostly because I have not judged myself by anyone else's standards or comparisons, but strictly by the standards of my own life. The idea to write this book was not contemplated over a long period of time. It came to me with inspiration and experiences led by a natural curiosity of life as well as a positive choice to share an earnest zest for living life, especially as our years increase. I can only hope that it will assist you as a companion for inspiration, a laugh, or something special that only you can see or understand. The ideas in this book are my chosen path. It is the way I intend to live until I reach the crossroads between the physical now and the big magical unknown.

The intention in writing this book has come from the best experiences in living life despite some of its darkest storms. This book will be loved. It will also be unloved. I accept this with years of experience in knowing that no piece of art or creative work can be appreciated by all. Such is not the intention of this writing. The book is written with good vibes and the simple intention for living big. It encourages *Living Older* as a time to be the most authentic you that YOU can be.

I hope to know many of you who are on this journey and I hope to hear your beautifully unique stories in *Living Older* as we meet at the **WOWAGEING**™ seminars and its other platforms of opportunities for communication and connection. Please come visit us at wowageing.com and join our community in *Living Older*. I look forward to connecting with you there.

I intend to write many more works on this passionate topic as well as other stories. Meanwhile, there is a lot of life to experience with a lot of buried opportunities to discover. Big love and journey on!

Take good care,
Lara Jay Hequet   iliveolder@wowageing.com

Make your choice and join us. Please check our calendar and schedule of seminars, courses and workshops at: **www.wowageing.com** For requests to speak in your community, please contact us at community@wowageing.com for more information and for our whereabouts.

Appendix

A Collection of More Ideas for Change Towards Living Older

Appendix i

New Dictionary for WOWAGEING™

Adventure in Living Older
Taking a big step forwards by doing something you have not done before.

Aloner
An individual who chooses to be alone so as to enjoy one's own company, to reflect on Self and the surrounding environment, to feel the connection with the soul and its bigger purpose and to be with the Universe and all of its powers.

Ambulance Relationship
A relationship of neediness that requires a lot of special care from one or more of the individuals within the relationship resulting in an imbalance of conscious energy for any of the people involved.

Blame Baggage
The accumulation of reasons to blame one or more people in your relationships for what you did not get for your Self. This becomes very addictive because it is an easy thing to do and before you know it, you have collected a heavy weight that strains the fluidity in living a big life.

Bombardistically
An adverb to accompany any situation designed to keep you addicted to its messages. These situations appear with a 'loud silence' that is usually very attractive to experience.

Burden-Loaded
A heavy and an imposing condition that is a result of accumulating a lot of negative feelings and criticisms from the Self or from other people.

Buy-Buy-Buy World

A world that is designed around acquiring things and more things, in the hope of making us remain within the illusion of constant happiness, even if it means being caught in debt for things you do not really need.

Chief Approval Officer

Also known as, an individual's innate wisdom and awareness of one's own mind and body. It is most appropriately used in the context of what foods serve you best as your unique Self evolves through the many adventures of life.

Evolver

A practice or an idea that will inspire and guide us in the Art of Living Older. Thoughts and practices that are continuous, the designs and outcomes of which will be different for each individual.

Experiential Allure

A glow that is warm and 'uplifting'. It accompanies an act you choose to courageously perform with the collaboration of all the positive energy within you and surrounding you. When you acquire it, you feel like a fan club in the Universe is cheering you on. Warning: Only those with special 'super powers' can see it. It also accompanies the choice you make to place your Self on the path of many life adventures instead of hiding from them.

Fashionise

To create individual expression that is so cool, everyone wants to try it.

Feeling-In-The-Mouth

A condition that takes over when the mouth takes priority over every other sense in the body.

Growing Older

A way of being established by set behaviours that revolves continuously in the same way through the entirety of a life. This includes being an expert at repetitive and conditioned behaviour, even if it is of no service to Self and others.

This way of being narrows down possibilities and options, often excluding an interest in the unknown. Such a way of living results in becoming and remaining a monolithic kind of creature throughout the journey of a beautiful living life, as if you were a king or queen of the comfort zone.

Les Nouveaux Métiers

French – New professions. In the context of this book, it would be used to explain new professions in terms of possibilities and and creativity in *Living Older*.

Life Designers

Consciously styling the choices you make in living the life you own.

Living Older

A way of being that requires practice and consciousness to cultivate a uniqueness of purpose through the entirety of a life. This includes all of the senses: seeing, smelling, hearing, tasting, touching, and understanding every situation, adventure and experience as if for the very first time, every time. This way of being allows the body, the mind and the emotions to relearn and re-evaluate each new situation with a sense of wonder and curiosity, equalling the magic of 'first times'. Living continuously in such a way throughout the multi-faceted experiences of our life journey is like being a king or queen of the thrill of uncertainty. *Living Older* is a way of looking forwards more than it is a way of looking backwards.

Olderness

A state of being that is manifested with repetition of acts or ways of being that do not serve a conscious purpose but continue to remain the same and never change despite the increasing years in life or the changing environments.

Pharoosh

An expression made with the energy of sound to add dramatic effects to a situation that leaves you in a perplexed wonder as to how we as human beings sometimes misbehave in regards to Self, other people, the environment that surrounds us and the planet we live in.

Photostorygrapher

A person who tells stories using pictures taken with a whole lot of passion but without any professional knowledge or skill.

Phuckploration

An act that involves exploiting the earth and its resources to satisfy the insatiable greed of some humans. This destructive action creates negative consequences and serious loss for the larger number of living beings including both human and non-human whose rights to live on an unexploited planet are taken away without knowledge, awareness and consent.

Purpose-Trators

People who will spread some goodwill, love, positivity, knowledge and skill for the benefit of all living beings, including the planet, as a part of their life purpose.

Resexatate™

An act that requires stretching the limited concept of sex to wider ideas and ways of being for those who no longer need to procreate. It includes fun, respect, passion, creativity and a whole lot of sensuality.

Sheep Language

A repetitive language of limitation that prevents a person from achieving what they really want to do for fear of being 'disliked'.

Therefore, one just follows and does what the larger group of 'others' are doing. Note: Absolutely, no disrespect meant to any sheep.

Splashers
People who make things happen in the course of their lives. They make positive change happen. They create WOW factors.

Soakers
People who prefer to sit on the sidelines to watch change as it happens. They have strong abilities to criticise what they will not try to do. They may also sit down and wish a lot.

The Noise
Some types of media or entertainment that may choose to provide limited and one-sided information that serves them more than it serves the rest of mankind and Nature.

Wait-Until-You-Die
An abnormal phenomenon surrounding a person who is left with no more purpose to contribute to another life on this planet, and just waits for the end of his/her life to come.

Wearing a Silver Head
The art of wearing grey, silver or white hair with an aura and allure of awesomeness.

What-if-ers
People who are afraid to move forwards; therefore, they surround themselves with justifications of "what-if" questions.

What The Farfallas!
An exclamation of utter astonishment that creates a flurry of butterflies every time it is exclaimed.

Wild Soul
A soul that is in a conscious connection with the physical Self as it journeys the life it is given here.

WOWAGEING™
A positive movement that commits to replace growing older with The Art of Living Older. This movement includes a worldwide community of like-minded people who intend to *Live Older*. Be a part of the movement at wowageing.com

WOWAGER™
A unique and beautiful individual, who is also a member of the **WOWAGEING™** movement.

Wrinkle Wrapping
It is an act that shames the natural design and purpose of wrinkles.

Appendix ii

A New Financial Plan

A Home. Small but sufficient for you, a partner, a dog, a cat and two other members possibly in transition. Easy to clean and maintain. Keeps you warm and cool accordingly. Always enough space for visitors.

Land. To lay your head on the grass and to walk about barefoot and naked, if you choose to do so. To grow some vegetables and fruit trees that will feed you and some others.

Temporary homes. That you do not own but can reside in as you travel.

Exchange spaces. With other life travellers as you travel from place to place.

A good support. From a cluster of like-minded people.

A little cash. To invest in the ability to learn something new.

A little cash. To afford very few passionate hobbies and interests.

Always enough food. And drink to share with all sorts of people with a zest for life and its many stories.

Enough cash. To travel.

Real food. That is clean and grown according to Nature's requirements.

Acquire many skills. That you can use when required.

Les Nouveaux Métiers: A Creative New Industry for Purposeful Work in Living Older

1. Market Vendor

You can criticise, analyse and advise a whole lot of people for free whilst making some money selling sustainable and wholesome produce or artisanal crafts. The energy here is mostly vibrant. There are always many people at markets with whom you can connect.

2. Busker

It is never too late to sing, dance and perform on the streets. You have nothing to be embarrassed about. Once you get over the jitters, it is warming for the soul, yours and maybe some others. It is not about acceptance from your possible spectators. It is about empowering yourself to step into 'new shoes'.

3. A Match Maker

Make love happen by bringing people together.

4. Happiness Ambassador

Choose to light up the immediate people around you with simple tokens of pleasure such as your fun company, your welcome assistance, your bright smile, your warm hug; keep thinking of more...

5. Chief Play Group Organiser

Encourage like-minded people from your community to get together to play with movement. After all, some people think you are almost senile anyway... Get communities to start creating 'Adult Play-Grounds' for recreational play.

6. Whole Foods Prep Artist
Feeding the younger 'rat racers' better foods as they run around chasing paper and money.

7. Grower of Wild Foods
Grow your own wild foods. Adopt a busy person and sell it to them. You will be an important part in supplying a much-needed demand.

8. A Story Teller in Public Spaces
Use your voice to create stories that inspire and make people feel good. No equipment required.

9. Create a New Language
Speak it with people you do not know. Learn from their reactions and expand your creativity. If they are closed-minded, they will give you a look and assume you are senile anyway! Meanwhile, you get to enjoy the energy that comes with stretching your creativity to new and unknown levels.

10. Mentor for Children
Children other than your own, with stories that are waiting to be heard and felt.

11. Integrate with the Youth of
your community and farther. Share conversations, skills and the energy to create something out of nothing with them.

12. Vintage Photostorygrapher
Your eye has a special story to tell. It is individual to you. It is full of the contradictions that life has danced around you.

Appendix iv

Curious Questions Concerning the Concept of Old

Skills and Olderness. Where is the real problem?

Are older people too stubborn to update and to invest in new skills?

What if older people are more flexible and reliable?

Would older people be more valuable if they were topped up with more experience, than a younger work force?

Besides, why is there competition rather than complementation?

What if new work that is relevant and has more purpose were created?

What if there was life outside of the corporate and capital ideal work force?

What if it were a sector called the **Purpose-Trators**?

Why are we not creating work full of passion for those who will continue to work and to contribute to important purposes?

In some communities the elders are engaged to clear up dirty tables at food centres and to clean public toilets. What does this say about a community's consciousness in regards to their elders? Is this exploitation of the elders or is it a financial opportunity limited to the elders?

Appendix v

Change in Business Ideas

Creating worth in young and older people.

What do these two demographics have in common? Big change, endless possibilities and a strong need to leave a mark.

Create a template for a new accounting system in the journey of life. A business requires accountability, why not a well-lived life?

Create a small business of value that fulfils moral demands and supplies integrity.

Spend your money with awareness and consciousness.

In a world of quiet chaos, you need a mixture of two opposing forces: a splurge of rushed energy and an even-paced energy of innate calmness, to create a perfect balance in a partnership for anything.

Appendix vi

Forms of Art vs. Forms of Compliance

Wear 'Grey/Silver' hair like a unique sculpture.

Colour hair for decoration not as a camouflage.

If your hair growth is weak, shave it and decorate your head as an art form worn as a crown.

Reject all forms of compliance or comparisons to how you once looked.

Clothes be creative and challenged in expressing your Self with very few items of quality and comfort using your sensuality as influence.

Lift your head up. Roll your shoulders back. Own the walk of *Living Older*.

Speak with distinction. Roll words out of your mouth that come from your soul. Treat your words and thoughts as priceless wealth.

Celebrate any healthy and legal crazy idea that you come up with, even if it does not provide you with results you needed right away.

Unleash your individual creativity and let your soul express itself.

Do not seek love and appreciation from outside of your Self, first.

Learn to sprinkle 'love dust' on haters. You may start a contagious way-of-being.

Appendix vii

A Letter To the Inspirational Wild Souls who are Living Older

Dearest Souls,

I do not know all of you. Some of you I have met in passing at unexpected times on the streets as I travel to different places. Some of you I have met for a brief greeting. Although I do not know you, I admire your choice in *Living Older*. The individuality you all possess has nothing in common. Like true art, some have more colour, others are more black and white.

What you do share in common has been your continuous big life in your increasing years. I know now that it is not the easiest thing to do, but it is certainly far from impossible. You show me very often that narrowed lines are just a thought one can measure when sitting on a chair in a room. It is the art and practice in stretching them out, outside of chairs and rooms that holds my interest. I know

it is difficult. Then again, with the experience in living, has not attaining a good life always been a mixture of easy and difficult?

I am attempting to share a message that 'increasing years' is not as bad and as miserable as the world has made it out to be. I can only hope that we, each and every one of us, awaken to our own unique dance in *Living Older*. In so doing, perhaps we create a better-lit path to life for the generations following us.

As I journey my fifties, I am fascinated by the endless possibilities I still see. These did not somehow 'fall upon me with great fortune'. I have not spent my lifetime accumulating material wealth. My thrill has been in living a hands-on life, similar to digging for artefacts from the deepest earth without a fixed map and plan.

I know there must be many more people who experience the same sentiments about life as we live it in our many different ways. I am writing this letter to let you know that we are inspired by you. Even though, our earthly journeys are not identical, I believe our souls seek the same intentions.

Take good care and journey on with Peace, Love and Contentment,

Lara Jay Hequet

About the Author

Lara Jay Hequet is an artistic mosaic of different ethnicities and global vibes. She speaks many languages and credits this gift to the ease in creating bridges with anyone or any place, and in not remaining different for too long.

She is a qualified chef, a certified holistic nutritionist, creator of the **WOWAGEING**™ movement, an adjunct professor, a professional restaurateur, an entrepreneur, a life traveller, a dedicated mother, a creative clinical aromatherapist, a good human being and mostly, an ordinary individual who surfs through the non-monotonous waves of life's incomparable beauty.

She intends to learn continuously and to be of use throughout her time on this planet. She believes that life is beautiful for the experiences that enrich us and for the connections we make in our entire lifetime, no matter the number in age or its condition. There is a lot she does not know. This allows her the opportunity to always have something to do and to discover. She is not perfect and she cherishes this way of being.

iliveolder@wowageing.com
wowageing.com

The Beginning

This book is only a beginning.
There will be many more.
Life is so full of living,
so do not be a bore.
There will be much giving,
sharing and mingling.
Maybe a dance or two
or a song good for a shoe.
The point is who cares
but You to live a life that bares.
I can do one little thing,
Many I's can do much more.
Be kind, be love,
Be what you need to be.
I hope to see you soon
At an event or two for you.
I know only what I know.
More importantly, like you
I will live a life that's true.

Acknowledgements

A journey towards the creation of a book includes many small and large adventures that become stories worthy of sharing. You will read some of these at www.righttowritepublishing.com/blog.

The same journey leads into life altering experiences when you decide to continue with the process required in the making of a book. This book has a positive energetic vibe of its own that became one with me as I persevered into the unknowns of an entirely new business.

Through random selection and some magic in the power of Universal attraction I have met many people who have assisted me in the production of this book from my raw and colourful manuscript to a version of ebook or print that you hold in you hand.

I take the opportunity to be in a heartfelt gratitude for all those who have now become a part of my team as well as those whose work was a temporary one. Your magic was never weighed in time spent but in the weight of your devotion.

Thank you Alexia for being my supporting light. You are proof that age is only a number. Your wisdom and eye for beauty encompasses your young age. I could not have completed this work of passion without your patient support, your heart-warming care and your love.

Thank you Kira for your generous advice. As I started my journey into the dark tunnel of publishing, you gave me a candle that led me in the right direction to some of the initial light switches.

Thank you Gary for your contribution. Caitlin, I thank you for being you, exactly as you are. I thank you for assuring that my unique voice agreed to marry some of the structured words in order to remain authentic within a foundation of better understanding for the reader.

Thank you Kuan, Jakub, Stanislaf and Addie for floating in and out of my initial experiences in the creation of *Once Upon A Time I Would Grow Old*. Thank you, Alexandra and Maximiliano for finding me in this huge Universe. I am honoured to be a part of your lives. Thank you for trusting in my vision as you listened to every crazy detail of my briefs and delivered the illustrations that I requested to match the visuals of my ideas.

Thank you, James, for trying the best that you could try and for not giving up until you could no longer.

Thank you, Saskia, for appearing and insistently reappearing into my life to do the work you were meant to do in partnering with my vision while we played in the sunshine of unlimited creativity as we breathed life into this book of passion.

Thank you, Anne, for your much needed perspective and cheerleading when it was beginning to get a little too difficult.

Most of all, I thank the positive energy of The Universe, my guide through this entire up-and-down-and-sideways squeeze of trials, and for providing me with more insight and experiences to be of purpose for my Self and for those who need your light in living the best life possible.

This book is made to
inspire your Self to
live the best life you
can design.
Absolutely no excuses!

A CIP catalogue record for this book is available upon request.

ISBN 978-981-09-4791-0

First Published by RIGHT TO WRITE PUBLISHING
www.righttowritepublishing.com

For information regarding assistance with publishing, please contact:
heart@righttowritepublishing.com

For orders of special gift prints and handcrafted hard cover binding, please contact: shop@wowageing.com

Right to WRITE
Publishing

London I Singapore